Unleashing the Millionaire Power of ChatGPT

Make More Money as a Beginner, Entrepreneur, or Business Owner with AI Chatbots & Custom Prompts

Boost Marketing, Productivity & Course Creation

FutureFront

Contents

Introduction

> *At least 40% of all businesses will die in the next 10 years... if they don't figure out how to change their entire company to accommodate new technologies.*
>
> — John Chambers, Cisco

Running a business these days is tough, isn't it? You need to keep creating new content and finding fresh information every day. At the same time, you're trying to improve your services for your clients, who could be anyone from individual customers to other companies. And if you're thinking about starting a new business or coming up with a fresh idea, the pressure is even more intense. With so much going on, it's no surprise you might feel the need for a super-helpful virtual assistant.

That's where ChatGPT comes in, ready to save your day and maybe even your whole business life. This amazing AI tool can help with everything we've talked about, and it's quickly becoming the go-to software for big-time entrepreneurs and corporate firms worldwide. ChatGPT can handle customer queries, generate business leads, and give you more time to focus on growing your business. You can even use it to boost your sales, just by giving it simple commands.

But before we dig into the nitty-gritty of ChatGPT, let's get a general idea about AI. We'll take a quick look at what AI is, where it comes from, what it's meant to do, and some myths about it. This will give you a better idea of how you can use the software to meet most of your company's needs.

The Rise of AI and ChatGPT

When the phrase "artificial intelligence" gets thrown around in conversation, most people automatically imagine a scenario where Skynet enslaves mankind. But did you consider putting a cap on the terminator's head and asking him about marketing pitches? Well, you can't do that yet, but ChatGPT is as close as it gets.

Let's take a trip down memory lane. The roots of AI can be traced back to the mid-20th century. This marked our initial encounter with artificial intelligence, as programmers began to equip computers with the ability to execute specific tasks through rule-based programming. Fast-forward to the present day, and AI has evolved dramatically. It's now capable of understanding and interpreting certain tasks, much like a human. In fact, AI has transformed into an indispensable ally. It steps in when we're fatigued or unable to perform certain tasks, effectively simplifying our lives and offering invaluable assistance.

AI has come a long way since its initial stages, where it was simply about machines following programmed instructions. This progress is largely attributable to the significant strides in computing power and data processing capabilities we possess today. A prime example of AI's recent advancements is the Generative Pre-trained Transformer systems, known as GPT. If that sounds familiar, it's because it forms the foundation of our star software, ChatGPT.

GPT is a type of neural language model, but let's avoid the technical jargon. Essentially, this software is trained with an immense amount of data, which enables it to generate text or responses that mimic human interaction. It communicates so convincingly that you might find yourself treating it like a colleague, explaining tasks as if to another person. But let's not forget, it's still just AI at the end of the conversation.

With ChatGPT being so good at learning as well as answering questions quickly, accurately, and efficiently, countless benefits and uses have come from the use of GPT artificially intelligent software. The best part is that the text and the information received from this AI are highly accurate, informative, and knowledgeable. Another benefit is the fact that the chatbot is super fast when it comes to generating responses. If we had to give an example, well, what would normally take someone a day to come up with can be delivered in a few seconds with the right use of the GPT model.

The bottom line is that even though we still don't know how much more we can do and what else is possible with this AI, what we do know for certain is that it has reshaped our understanding and use of technology. Right now, it is giving us far more of a boost than anything we could have expected.

As we delve into the functionality and usage of this chatbot, one attribute stands out conspicuously — ChatGPT is increasingly being dubbed as a potential "Google Killer." While this might seem like an overstatement, the reality is that this technology is rapidly transforming the way we search for information.

Consider the most significant tech breakthroughs that have revolutionized the global market, such as the advent of the internet and Google. Now, visualize something even more advanced. This AI technology is designed to precisely address your queries and deliver accurate responses, bypassing the need to sift through a multitude of search results that might not contain the information you seek.

In essence, ChatGPT is set to become the 'next big thing,' the sought-after solution that everyone will want to utilize. If it surpasses Google in terms of efficiency and utility, it will truly be a comparison of apples to oranges, with nothing else coming close.

According to new information from BBC (Kleinman, 2023), the company tried out the ChatGPT chatbot AI software and found it very beneficial. They also stated that the technology is so advanced that you can get the chatbot to write you any sort of article, or give you insight on a certain topic. You can ask for ideas, content, research, and so much more. The BBC employees tried to get the chatbot to write an article to suit the company's style, but it responded that it was unable to do so without the right prompts to help facilitate it writing it in that specified style. This goes to show how advanced the chatbot is: It can tell you whether it can write a piece of information or an article that is similar to a certain website's content.

Can Google do this? Well, it can't. But then, that is not the end of Google. They, too, have been trying out new technology and have developed their own AI software, "Bard." They've incorporated this AI into their search engine software. If not, a lot of their users would be using the chatbot for more accurate and direct answers to their questions. It's only a matter of time before all the current search engines become obsolete due to the power of AI chatbots. The Bard AI is conceptually the same as ChatGPT; however, when you use it, it does notify you that it is in its experimental stage. It is not yet a part of the Google search engine, but it is almost about to replace the Google Assistant (Martindale, 2023).

Similar to this information is the recent announcement from Microsoft that they have incorporated the ChatGPT model into their search engine, Bing. ChatGPT was integrated into the search engine in February 2023 (Mehdi, 2023). They were onto the fact that their search engine may not be able to stand a chance alone, without any AI to help their users find answers quickly, efficiently, and accurately. Now, users flock to Bing to get the direct answers and results they need.

Imagine it: If huge companies like Google and Microsoft see the need for AI, it's only natural that we should also look for ways to get the most out of this new artificially intelligent software.

The Potential of ChatGPT for Entrepreneurs, Beginners, and Business Owners

As we've discussed, the benefits of ChatGPT extend far beyond mere content provision and question answering. This AI software unlocks a myriad of opportunities for businesses to level up. From lead generation and customer support to market research and content creation, the sky is the limit. Moreover, it assists in streamlining operations and amplifying sales by prioritizing customer satisfaction. While this is just a summary, the key takeaway is that ChatGPT can significantly enhance your business's revenue generation. Let's briefly touch upon some ways in which it can do so. Rest assured, we'll delve into each of these aspects more comprehensively in the following chapters.

- **Customer Service:** ChatGPT can revolutionize your customer service by addressing queries and providing support. This can reduce call and email volumes, translating into significant cost savings. What's more, by delivering top-notch customer service, you can ignite word-of-mouth promotion, ultimately boosting sales and expanding your client base.
- **Sales and Marketing:** Keeping a finger on the pulse of emerging trends is crucial in marketing. ChatGPT makes it effortless to identify top-selling products and customer favorites. Along with the chatbot, you also get

software that enables you to tailor messages and marketing pitches, potentially turbocharging your sales leads.

- **Market Research:** ChatGPT can analyze vast amounts of data to provide insights about market trends, customer preferences, and competitors, which can be instrumental in making informed business decisions that could lead to increased revenue.
- **Content Generation:** One of ChatGPT's primary uses is generating content. From blog posts, articles, and social media content to emails and newsletters, ChatGPT can do it all. This reduces the need for outsourcing and speeds up the content production process, helping businesses save money and potentially increasing revenue by boosting their digital presence.
- **Product Development:** ChatGPT can be used to gather feedback from customers and provide suggestions for product enhancements. This iterative process of improvement can lead to better products, higher sales, and more satisfied customers.
- **Employee Development:** ChatGPT can be an invaluable tool for supplying employees with targeted training and development resources. This boosts productivity, equips them with specific skills, and enhances their understanding of various systems. The resultant cost savings on training workshops and other expenses, along with the improved employee performance, can lead to larger profit margins and higher retention rates.

- **Process Automation:** ChatGPT can automate certain repetitive tasks, such as invoice processing and report generation. Thanks to the AI's efficiency and accuracy, you save both time and labor costs.

This list goes on! We'll look into this further and see how you can transform a chatbot into a tool as important as a multi-talented and expert virtual assistant for your business.

Overview

This book is your comprehensive guide to understanding AI and how it can drive your business to success, regardless of the industry. Harnessing the power of ChatGPT, you can leverage its advantages to amplify sales and income with a remarkably simple solution. You'll discover a multitude of ways to integrate the benefits of this chatbot into your business as we delve deeper into the world of this advanced AI tool.

Importantly, you don't need to be a tech whizz or have any prior knowledge of software or artificial intelligence. This book is designed to equip you, whether you're tech-savvy or not, with all the essential information you'll need to start reaping the benefits of this chatbot for yourself and your business. You'll learn how ChatGPT can enhance your existing business and propel it forward with course and book creation, content creation ideas, market research, and even launching new businesses using the AI chatbot. Additionally, you'll pick up valuable tips on integrating ChatGPT with your blog, website, or company platform, either directly or using a ChatGPT plugin.

Empowered with knowledge and confidence, you'll be prepared to leverage ChatGPT to its full potential, ensuring it works tirelessly to aid you and your business in today's fast-paced landscape. You'll be better equipped to handle the relentless demands of the business world, as this AI tool can address most of your needs.

But before you dive in and start experimenting with this incredible chatbot, let's first brush up on some basic theories of artificial intelligence.

Chapter 1
A Short Brief on Artificial Intelligence

You've already had a taste of artificial intelligence in the introduction, but let's delve a little deeper. We'll explore more about the topic and trace its roots to better understand where it all began. Let's get into the history of artificial intelligence, what we're doing with artificial intelligence now, and where artificial intelligence will take us in the future (Hunt, 2021).

A Look Into the Past

When it comes to the history of anything, there is always a rich culture and information to help us understand, learn from, and revere the past. It's the same story with artificial intelligence.

The origins of AI can be traced back to the mid-20th century. Computer scientists began to investigate the concept of machine intelligence. Eventually, the Dartmouth Conference was founded in 1956 by John McCarthy, Marvin Minsky,

Claude Shannon, and Nathan Rochester. This is well-known as the birthplace of artificial intelligence (Schroer, 2023). Back then, the conference of researchers had the idea to create intelligent machines that could eventually perform tasks that required human intelligence, such as problem-solving and decision-making. From this point onward, researchers began developing programs and systems to simulate human intelligence.

Artificial intelligence is a rapidly evolving field based on two principles: ancient philosophy and mathematics. The modern history of AI, on the other hand, describes how, in the early years of AI research, the emphasis was on developing symbolic AI systems that used rules and symbols to perform tasks. This was the first type of AI that was mentioned earlier—the type that could only ever follow the commands it was given.

It was during the 1960s and 1970s that AI researchers made astounding advances in expert systems and natural language processing. Then again, it was at this point that the AI systems' limitations became apparent. These limitations did not deter the researchers; rather, they encouraged them to try new approaches.

Connectionism—also known as neural networks—emerged in the 1980s. The human brain inspired this new approach to AI. The researchers intended to use a neural network system that was composed of interconnected nodes to help the artificial intelligence system learn from data and adapt to new information. This method was extremely useful, particularly in image and speech recognition applications. Shortly after this, interest in AI waned due to a lack of funding and so on.

The 1990s, however, witnessed a resurgence of interest in artificial intelligence as computing power started evolving rapidly. This was largely driven by steady advancements in computing capacity, algorithms, and data. This period held a significant place in human evolution - albeit through machines. Artificial intelligence started learning from data, focusing on algorithms, and consequently becoming increasingly efficient and intricate. In essence, some of these algorithms facilitated the development of a range of applications including natural language processing, computer vision, and recommendation systems - all of which we'll explore further later on.

Following that, in the early 2000s, a new branch of artificial intelligence came into being - deep learning via neural networks. This employed multilayered neural networks to learn complex data representations. Deep learning was a game-changer in the AI sphere, enabling breakthroughs in numerous areas like speech recognition, natural language understanding, and image recognition.

Today, AI finds applications in a host of professional and personal spheres. From powering self-driving cars to aiding in medical treatment and diagnosis, the possibilities are limitless. However, despite AI's myriad successes, it still grapples with considerable challenges that act as obstacles to its wider adoption, especially in sectors where trust is paramount. Nevertheless, researchers are undeterred, persisting in their quest for the ultimate AI.

To summarize this history lesson, we must realize that there has been significant progress in the development of AI, as well as challenges that were too difficult to address in one go. Nonetheless, AI has come a long way since it was merely a concept. It is now a critical component of technology, with applications in a wide range of industries.

Despite this, as AI evolves, it is critical to be upfront and address the challenges to the professional field that everyone must be aware of so that they, and all of us, can ensure that AI is used responsibly.

Let's take a closer look at how it works and what it actually is now.

What Is It?

AI, or Artificial Intelligence, replicates human intelligence in machines that are programmed to think, learn, and carry out tasks that usually necessitate human intelligence. It covers a wide array of subfields like machine learning, natural language processing, computer vision, and robotics, to name a few. AI technologies are engineered to scrutinize data, identify patterns, make decisions, solve problems, and automate tasks, all with differing levels of autonomy.

How Does AI Work?

Because it isn't yet 100% human-like, it works by using algorithms that learn from data fed into them—or, to put it another way, AI learns as you program it. How the AI system can predict or decide on a specific scenario is entirely based on this data.

Let's take a closer look at the cognitive abilities that artificial intelligence employs to complete these tasks.

- **Learning processes** refer to an AI's ability to learn from its experiences. It can learn through either supervised or unsupervised methods. When it comes to supervised learning, the AI system has been trained with labeled data, and the desired output is already known because it is simply returning what was received. Based on the data it has been provided, the system then learns to make predictions related to the question or the command. In the case of unsupervised learning, the AI system is trained using unlabeled data, and the outcome is unknown and unpredictable. The AI system learns to recognize patterns in data from whatever is fed into it.

- **Reasoning processes** are similar to the human brain, and involve an AI system's ability to make decisions or predictions using logic and reasoning. For this to work, a model of the world is created for it, and the AI must make assumptions based on the model. It will then have to provide an answer or draw a conclusion based on its assumptions. Keep in mind that reasoning can be deductive, inductive, or abductive. Almost human-like.

- **Self-correction processes** consider where the AI system starts learning from its mistakes and then begins correcting itself. It does this primarily by relying on feedback from its users or the environment and then adjusting its behavior accordingly.

Why is AI Important?

AI has the potential to solve complex problems, and it can, like any other machine, tool, or system, make our lives easier. Currently, artificial intelligence can directly improve healthcare, transportation, and education, among other areas of our lives, and this is because it can automate repetitive tasks, make data-driven predictions, generate accurate content, and assist us in making better decisions overall. If we had to think of it, personal and professional artificial intelligence is the next step in our evolution.

The Advantages and Disadvantages of AI

AI, like everything else in the world, has its advantages and disadvantages. This is inevitable, and we must learn to make use of the advantages while also learning to adapt to the disadvantages. First, let's look at the benefits:

- **AI is efficient.** As previously stated, AI can automate repetitive tasks such as email management, appointment scheduling, and even market research. We'll look into this later, but using AI to do these tasks will significantly reduce the time and effort required to complete them. It is beneficial to a company.
- **AI is accurate.** Based on the data fed to it, it can make predictions and decisions. This reduces the possibility of human error and any other unintentional errors. Most of the time, we as human beings overlook grammatical and spelling errors. After all, to err is

human. We may also respond to a question with incorrect information or values. This is not something that AI will do unless intentionally programmed or commanded to do so.

- **It's scalable.** AI is designed to process massive volumes of data with speed and precision. With the march of technology, it achieves this with minimal delay and error, making it invaluable for analyzing intricate systems. On the other hand, human capabilities have inherent boundaries. We can only absorb, retain, and process a limited amount of information simultaneously. Unlike our brains, which can become overwhelmed with too much data, AI excels at large-scale processing, designed specifically to handle such heavy-duty tasks.
- **It has 24/7 availability.** Because AI systems can work around the clock without needing to take a break, your systems can be online 24 hours a day, 7 days a week. They don't need to rest or eat, and this makes them ideal for tasks that require constant monitoring. The human workforce requires rest, food, and breaks to be productive, which demonstrates how beneficial implementing AI in the workplace can be. Artificial intelligences can do many things that we as humans would not be able to carry out because of our living bodies' needs. Super-powered AI does not have the same weaknesses we do.

The benefits of AI are indeed substantial, but it's crucial to also acknowledge its limitations. Despite its remarkable advancements, AI continues to grapple with significant hurdles, including:

- **Mistrust due to lack of transparency.** One of the most pressing concerns is the need for more explainable AI. As its systems become more complex, it can be difficult to understand how they arrived at a particular decision or recommendation. For people who want (or need) to know this information, this lack of transparency can be a barrier; this is especially prevalent in industries where trust is essential. This is cited as a common reason why people will refuse to integrate their business with AI.
- **Bias.** Another challenge confronting AI is the requirement for more diverse and inclusive data. AI systems perform only as well as the data they are trained on. Inaccurate or skewed data can produce biased outcomes, and to avert reinforcing existing inequalities, it's crucial to train AI on data sets that truly represent the diverse world we live in. Since AI lacks self-awareness, bias can creep in inadvertently at times. Efforts are being made to educate AI about these biases and curb potential misinterpretations, but it's a complex problem that requires ongoing attention.
- **Innate lack of empathy.** Remember that these systems do not feel or think the same way we do. For this reason, they lack empathy. Because artificial intelligences cannot empathize with humans, they are

less useful in situations requiring emotional intelligence.

- **Potential job losses.** Many jobs that were previously performed by humans can be automated by AI systems, which can work more efficiently and quickly, with no delays or human errors disrupting the workflow. This may eventually result in job losses. However, this is not the intention of AI. We must adapt to what artificial intelligences can do and learn what they cannot surpass human beings at. By also improving in our own fields and ensuring that we are capable of more than AI is, there will be no need to fear job loss.
- **Potential security risks.** AI systems could be vulnerable to takeover by cyberattacks. If they are used maliciously, it could result in a loss of time, completed work, and data (and, of course, money).

The benefits of AI are plentiful and, in general, surpass its drawbacks. When contemplating the integration of AI, it's pragmatic to strategize how to tackle potential issues or devise solutions for any side effects arising from system use. For instance, not relying entirely on AI, but instead incorporating human supervision, can accelerate work completion and provide a safety net against possible cyber threats.

With that said, let's now turn our attention to the various types of artificial intelligence that are prevalent today.

Four Types of AI

Most of us assume that AI is AI, and only comes in one form. In actuality, there are four different types of AI, which include:

Reactive Machines

These systems, reminiscent of the earliest forms of AI, operate strictly based on specific instructions. They lack the ability to learn or store information, focusing purely on executing assigned tasks and reacting to direct inputs.

Theory of Mind

Artificial intelligences of this kind demonstrate an ability to understand and predict human mental states. They process inputs such as symptoms, feelings, and behavioral patterns to discern potential causes.

Self-Awareness

Self-aware AI systems denote a significant leap from the previous AI types. These entities possess a conscious sense of their own existence, much like human self-awareness. They understand their mental states, moving beyond mere reactionary behavior to their surroundings.

Limited Memory

AI systems of this type utilize past experiences and data to inform predictions or decisions. They are capable of learning from the data they interact with. However, their understanding doesn't extend to complex concepts.

ChatGPT aligns with the "Limited Memory" category of AI. It has been trained on extensive volumes of text data, which it uses to generate human-like text based on the inputs it receives. While it can't independently recall past interactions or learn from them, it generates pertinent responses by identifying patterns and structures in the data on which it was trained.

However, it is crucial to note that within the context of a single conversation, ChatGPT can maintain a temporary memory, enabling it to provide responses that are consistent with the ongoing dialogue. This feature does not permit it to store or remember information after the conversation ends, assuring users of their privacy and data security.

The ultimate goal in AI development is to achieve a system that integrates all the existing types of AI, culminating in a self-aware entity. The ideal AI would be able to carry on effortless conversations, understand humor, empathy, emotions, and encapsulate the complex range of human attributes. Reaching this milestone will signify the creation of a perfect piece of AI.

Next, we will explore how AI is being utilized across various professional fields, transforming traditional operations.

Applications of AI

AI has a wide range of applications across various industries. Some are expected, while others are less so—many people would never expect AI to be responsible for so much effort and production. Let's look into these amazing uses now (Application of AI - Javatpoint, n.d.).

- **Agriculture:** AI is used in agriculture to analyze all crop data and then optimize crop yield and detect pests and diseases. Planting and harvesting tasks can also be performed by AI-powered agricultural robots. These machines are programmed to carry out a specific command, and they will do so.
- **Astronomy:** AI assists in the analysis of massive amounts of astronomical data. This data includes images of the sky as well as analyses and predictions about the compositions of various celestial objects. AI can also help with identifying and classifying unknown extraterrestrial objects. For example, we may not be able to determine the composition of a distant asteroid, but AI can calculate its size, rotation, route, and other factors. AI can make accurate predictions if given the necessary information.
- **Data security:** AI is capable of detecting and preventing cyber threats early. AI-powered security systems can detect anomalies as well as identify potential security breaches.
- **E-commerce:** AI is used in e-commerce to personalize product recommendations. It can also aid in pricing

optimization and the detection of fraudulent activity. Chatbots powered by AI can also provide customer support and respond to user queries quickly and efficiently.

- **Education:** By analyzing student data and detecting learning difficulties, AI is used to personalize learners' learning experiences. AI-powered educational apps can also provide an interactive learning experience, allowing students to improve their skills and comprehension much quicker and easier than before. The world is constantly changing, and education is no exception. Without the assistance of AI, many would struggle to meet the demands of today's education.

- **Entertainment:** In the entertainment industry, AI is used to create personalized content for users. It can then recommend new movies, TV shows, and music based on this information. AI-powered systems can also create realistic virtual worlds for gaming and other entertainment applications.

- **Finance:** Artificial intelligence can analyze financial data, detect fraud, and forecast market trends. Some AI-powered financial models can assist investors in making more informed decisions while also ensuring profits.

- **Gaming:** Artificial intelligence is fantastic at creating intelligent game characters. They can adapt to a player's behavior and provide users with a more immersive gaming experience. AI can also be used to optimize game graphics in game development. The main advantage is that AI helps to improve game performance.

- **Healthcare:** In the healthcare industry, artificial intelligence is used to analyze medical data. It is also used for the diagnosis of certain diseases and the development of treatment plans for them. There have also been advancements in AI-powered medical devices, such as wearable sensors that can monitor vital signs and detect potential health issues.
- **Robotics:** Separate from AI, this is one side of technology that deals with constructing, designing, and operating robots. Hardware AI is used in robotics to build intelligent robots that can perform tasks on their own. These robots are primarily employed in the manufacturing and healthcare industries, among others.
- **Social media:** In social media, AI is used to analyze user data. Furthermore, these systems personalize content and detect fake news. Chatbots powered by AI can also provide customer service and answer user questions. This has made e-commerce and other similar online uses much easier for small business owners to manage.
- **Travel and transport:** AI is used to optimize transportation routes and GPS navigation because it can predict traffic patterns and improve travel experiences. Similarly, AI is behind self-driving cars. AI-powered systems can also assist airports with luggage management and security.

AI's practical applications continue to broaden, becoming increasingly advantageous for businesses across nearly all sectors. As the technology advances, AI is becoming an essential tool for streamlining workflows and enhancing operational efficiency.

Over the years, AI has made considerable strides in supporting a wide array of industries, from manufacturing and business to healthcare and entertainment. It is leveraged to analyze vast data sets and make accurate predictions, an ability beyond the reach of human capabilities, and accomplished without human-induced delays or effort.

The evolution of AI is truly remarkable, and most importantly, it shows no signs of stopping. These systems will persist in their evolution, becoming increasingly sophisticated over time. Eventually, we could be holding a super AI system in our hands, achieving an equilibrium between organic and artificial beings for the greater benefit of the world and its inhabitants.

Having traced the history of AI and appreciated its present advancements, it's time to delve into our next chapter, which focuses on ChatGPT. This cutting-edge AI system has been making headlines across various media outlets, and it's the primary reason you're here. Let's discover what makes ChatGPT such an intriguing subject.

Chapter 2
ChatGPT

Before delving deeper into ChatGPT, its history, its benefits, and how we can apply them to your business, we must first take a closer look at language models and how they work. This is so that you can better understand how ChatGPT works and what makes it unique (Bednarski, 2023).

Language Models

As the name implies, a language model is a type of AI system that can both understand and generate human language. To put it another way, artificial intelligences that use language models can recognize patterns and relationships in text data in the same way that words can form sentences (Lee, 2023).

The Uses of Language Models

Language models offer numerous benefits and use-cases. Designed to comprehend our communications and inquiries, they can recognize speech, function as chatbots, and even operate as virtual assistants.

You might wonder how these models can acquire such knowledge and produce impressive content and assistance. The secret lies in their continuous learning from extensive datasets. Examples of these data sources include books and transcripts, which embody written or spoken language. Once trained, a language model AI can generate the required text by predicting what kind of output it should produce based on the input it has received. This capability renders the system so human-like that it's easy to forget you're interacting with an AI, not another person.

From the information shared so far, you should have a clear understanding of what ChatGPT is. As a language model birthed by the GPT-3 system, its primary function is to converse with users, providing accurate and relevant information in various written formats, ranging from code and blog posts to song lyrics and poetry. Thanks to its ability to process input and respond with vast amounts of precise data, the chatbot can even serve as a virtual assistant.

Beyond ChatGPT, language models are currently employed for the following purposes:

Search Engines

As previously stated, language models possess the ability to comprehend your queries and supply pertinent information in response. Consequently, you, as the searcher, don't have to navigate through numerous websites or sift through various articles to find the information you need. You can acquire what you seek in just a matter of seconds. Not only does the AI conserve time, but it also furnishes you with relevant information. Because they are superbly equipped to manage such tasks, language models are poised to revolutionize the world's search engines, delivering precise and pertinent information within seconds.

We can see some of these improvements on Bing. However, you still need to check your facts since there can be instances where the language model may not have the latest information about a certain event or situation. For example, there was a cutoff date on the recent information given to ChatGPT: It does not know much about recent events. There are moments when the AI will give you the wrong information, and this will not be related to what it was trained on. These hallucinations do occur (Gungor, 2023). The issue is that they may cause many people to no longer trust the system, as they will choose to go back to using search engines and the old-fashioned method of doing research.

Dynamic Bots as Artificially Intelligent Assistants

Language models can also serve as virtual assistants to help with answering customer inquiries and even scheduling appointments because they can understand the content being provided, predict the type of relevant information needed, and complete and fulfill the tasks required by the user. They learn almost as much as humans do and use a lot of information to come up with their responses and ensure that they're assisting you.

Life Science Research

Because these language models are constantly fed large amounts of data and information, they can analyze scientific data. The language model can then derive a reason for the cause and predict insights into treatments for specific health conditions. We also saw how they can assist with calculations regarding objects in space; AI can help us identify things we don't even know about.

Software Development

Language models already understand how to write code because they have information from written data and content. As a software developer, this will be extremely beneficial because the chatbot will be able to provide you with the correct code for specific functions. You will be able to focus on many complex tasks instead.

Smart Writing

In the context of ChatGPT, smart writing involves the AI leveraging advanced language generation capabilities to augment the clarity and consistency of the text it produces. This mechanism enables the AI to generate intelligent and comprehensible responses during a conversation. The proficiency of language model AI in text generation is so remarkable that it can be employed to craft a wide variety of content, and even be utilized for predictive typing.

Let's look at some of the aspects of smart writing now.

- **Context awareness:** This is where the AI will take into consideration the previous messages which you (the user) exchanged with it, and from that information it will understand what was said and then generate relevant and coherent responses.

- **Coherence models:** These models are designed in such a way that they are able to capture and understand the logic structure as well as the flow of a conversation. From this the AI is able to come up with responses which are relevant to what was asked and appropriate to the conversation.

- **Language fluency:** This is where the AI is trained with a lot of data so that it is able to respond with information that is grammatically correct and looks as though it was written by a human.

- **Error correction and fallback mechanisms:** This is a sort of failsafe where, if the AI responds with content that is not correct or coherent, the fallback mechanism will identify the mistakes and give feedback on this so that whatever is being written will at least make some sense and be helpful to you.

- **Semantic understanding:** This is where the AI will be able to understand what your question or statement means, and from this understanding it will be able to provide you with the correct information that you need. This is all done using semantic analysis, where the AI will be able to comprehend whatever was written and then come up with accurate information. This is how AI is able to come up with understandable responses to any statement or question you provide as input.

It's important to note, however, that there is a slight drawback to language models: they may not always provide the precise information you seek without first receiving a well-structured input or query. Though this may seem challenging initially, it's not a difficult skill to master, and we'll delve deeper into this aspect later on. For now, it's time to delve deeper into the main point of this chapter: ChatGPT. The history and purpose of the chatbot are discussed, as well as how it can help you as an individual and a business owner (*How Does Chat GPT Work?*, 2023).

The Origin of ChatGPT

ChatGPT is an incredible artificially intelligent chatbot that was built on OpenAI's natural language processing model, the Generative Pre-trained Transformer 3, or GPT-3. It was released by OpenAI in November 2022. This company specializes in developing and advancing existing artificial intelligence technology, as well as making it available to researchers, businesses, and others who can benefit from it. Moreover, the chatbot was built to assist people with various types of written content and services. It was intended to supplement, rather than replace, the human workforce.

Before ChatGPT came about, OpenAI worked on other language models, such as GPT-2, which is a forerunner to GPT-3. This language model was primarily used for language generation tasks. It could also generate code in a variety of different programming languages.

Other AI-related technologies are currently being developed by OpenAI. Two examples of these technologies are robotics and computer vision, which is a field of study under technology where computers are enabled to understand, interpret, and come up with meaningful information from visual data, which includes videos as well as images. The list of ways in which artificial intelligence is currently being expanded goes on and on.

GPT-3, GPT-3.5, and GPT-4

As we've established, ChatGPT was created using the GPT-3 model. GPT-3 can communicate through text prompts, and it can also perform a variety of language-related tasks. These include writing essays, blog posts, articles, letters, and computer code. GPT-3 understands context and content and can provide useful information that is directly related to or relevant to the material under consideration. The best part is that it is constantly learning every day from the amount of data researchers feed it as well as the amount of data users feed it.

GPT-3.5 is an upgrade to GPT-3 that includes additional training data and fine-tuning techniques to help it perform even better.

The versions GPT-3 and 3.5 were the most recent and largest versions of the GPT series of language models until recently, but OpenAI has already prepared the next step of evolution, GPT-4. This model was developed to improve upon all the technological advancements of its predecessors. GPT-4 is a data-to-text language model, as opposed to GPT-3 and 3.5, which only dealt with text inputs.

GPT-4 is already far superior to GPT-3—it's on a completely different level. The main reason is that GPT-4 is significantly larger than GPT-3. When it comes to size, GPT-4 has around 1 trillion parameters, compared to GPT-3, which has only around 175 billion. Due to this increased processing power, it can handle more complex instructions than GPT-3.

This recent version also outperforms GPT 3.5. It can successfully run tasks that were too difficult and complex to process under GPT 3.5, and it can learn much more quickly. In other words, GPT-4 is more intelligent. It is also more dependable and creative, as it can write far more complex code than the other versions could. Finally, GPT-4 provides much safer responses than its predecessors, as its responses are not as biased or lacking in empathy when compared to GPT 3 and 3.5 (Butler, 2023). From this information, we can say that the GPT language models will only continue to improve as time goes on.

The disadvantage, however, of GPT-4 is that it requires more computational power to use. However, do note that if you're subscribed to the GPT system, you can use the GPT-4 language model. Another disadvantage is that all of these models weren't trained on very recent information: their data only dates as far back as 2021. That is, unless you use an app like WebChatGPT to acquire certain recent information.

ChatGPT in a Nutshell

ChatGPT was created to be an artificially intelligent system that could communicate and hold a conversation while performing tasks as a chatbot or virtual assistant. It, like its predecessors and other language models, works by generating responses to the input provided by the user. These responses are based on the conversation's context, as well as the chatbot's knowledge of language and common sense.

How It Works

Any AI chatbot makes use of a technique known as self-attention. This technique will help it focus on different parts of the input before analyzing and forecasting its responses, so what it says will make sense and be contextually appropriate to the input.

If you're starting a new conversation or training the AI, it may not understand exactly what you are asking, or it may not have information about specific places or people. In this case, it will ask you to tell it more, and it will learn when you do so. This is due to the OpenAI technique of "training language models to follow instructions with human feedback." There are three steps to this technique:

1. Supervised Fine Tuning

In this step, the model is trained using a dataset of examples that demonstrate how to generate responses to specific prompts. For example, similar to how a programmer enters code into software to make it function in a specific way, the same process occurs here so that the chatbot can allow certain commands when asked similar questions.

2. Reward Model

In this step, the model is trained to produce responses that receive positive feedback from a human evaluator. For example, after the AI answers a question, it will ask you if the answer was correct or if it was relevant to your search. To allow it to learn, you can respond with either positive or negative feedback.

3. Reinforcement Learning Model

In this case, the model is trained to produce responses that achieve a specific goal or objective after receiving certain prompts requesting information. For example, if you ask the model a random question, it will respond with an answer. When you ask for a difficult response, such as one that necessitates content creation or research, the model is achieving a specific goal or completing a task. You are speaking to it about a specific point, so be sure to communicate all you need to in this session or thread so that the chatbot understands and remembers whatever you are referring to.

The chatbot will learn as it speaks to you by following all of these models. By first telling it what you need by giving it all of the necessary information and then asking the question(s) using prompts that are concise and to-the-point, you will receive the required information.

What GPT Language Models Can Do

We've already discussed how these models can be used for a variety of purposes, ranging from chatbots and virtual assistants to content creation. Another great use is how they help with language translation and even marketing pitches and research. The uses are more than just a handful, but from what we can already see, the ChatGPT language model is also another step toward the next stage of AI evolution. How? This model learns as you speak to it and it is constantly developing and improving itself with new content, data, and information fed to it on a daily basis. This model serves as a stepping stone to becoming better at language models. It assists researchers in learning how to improve their technology so that they can improve AI until they reach the desired stage.

Let's have a look at the other things this chatbot is capable of doing (Mohmad, 2023).

Responding to a Variety of Language Outputs

The chatbot can comprehend a wide range of content and context. This is mainly due to the way the system was designed. First, it must analyze and comprehend the data pattern that is being fed to it. It will then provide you with information based on the data you have provided.

For example, you may give the chatbot a lot of content along with the prompt you are asking it, like asking for a financial report on the past decade to verify the fluctuation of the economy's values pre-COVID, during COVID, and now. You can give specifics about what you are looking for, etc. The chatbot will understand and provide you with the appropriate financial report. Note that it also does research.

Answering Questions

Because this is a chatbot, you can expect it to respond to questions. This is a much more advanced type of chatbot than the ones found on specific business websites, which are designed to give you specific information or ask for personal information that will be submitted to a human being to get the answer or assistance that you require. It is the language model that handles all of the work.

For example, if you own an insurance company and a customer has a question about the claims process, all they have to do is type their question into the ChatGPT-powered chatbot on your website. It can understand what the client is saying and then provide an answer or whatever other type of content is required.

Remember that the answer will be specific to the questions asked, and this does not mean simple questions either. The best part about this feature is that it can help businesses on a massive scale. After all, some customer queries these days aren't answered on a company's website, and most customers or clients prefer to speak with someone in person to get the help they require. As a result, the benefits of answering questions in a correct and informative manner will keep customers satisfied with their resolved queries, which are all dealt with quickly and efficiently. This will save you time, effort, and money that would have been spent otherwise had you used a regular workforce to manage such applications.

Providing Improved Interpretability of Information

Until recently, many people did not trust language models to respond to their questions or queries. But because it's so clear where ChatGPT gets the information and data it needs to answer your questions, it's much easier to trust it than previous language models. The reason is mainly because the chatbot will not come up with information from its own intuition or guesses. Everything is factual, and comes from sources available to you on the internet: literature, articles, and other publicly-available sources of written content. The chatbot also does not utilize any sources of information that are not available to the public. This makes the ChatGPT far more suitable for real-world applications than other chatbots.

Users can converse with ChatGPT, and it will answer in an honest manner. Obviously, the AI isn't programmed to lie, and so if you ask it where it is getting its information or research from, you will get the answer. For example, if you had to ask the earlier chatbots a question about specific brands or companies, you would not get the same information as you would from ChatGPT, which learns from users as well as other written and visual content. You might be given information that was potentially biased or incorrect in some way.

Acting as an Alternative to Google Search

As previously stated, the chatbot is quickly becoming known as the "Google Killer." This is due to the fact that many people believe the language model is more efficient and better suited to serve as a search engine. The reason for this is that the chatbot does not provide you with a selection of links to various search results. Instead, it provides you with the direct and correct response you require.

For example, if you type "Who was responsible for the Trojan War?" into Google, you'll get a variety of answers. You will receive a lot of information about the attack and the war, with links taking you to specific pages to get these details, but not all of it will give you a straightforward answer with a start-to-finish story. In the end, you will likely search through the Wikipedia link and then some other articles to get what you need. But ChatGPT will instead give you a summary of who was responsible for the war, how the person in charge orchestrated the attack using the Trojan Horse, and how it affected the victims who fell for the plot.

Writing High-Performing Copy

We'll look into this ability in detail further on, but this chatbot is perfectly capable of writing copy. Email, marketing campaigns, newsletters, articles, ad copy, and other forms of communication are all examples of this.

You could ask the chatbot to write a marketing copy for your company X, which is developing and marketing a high-end shower gel. In a matter of seconds, you will be provided with excellent and unique copy for your brand.

The trick is to use prompts with correct and factual information to help the chatbot understand what you require and which information to include in your material. We'll go over some of these prompts later on as well as how to write them. The chatbot can generate copy that resonates with target audiences and drives engagement by analyzing large amounts of text data and identifying patterns in language usage. This is especially useful for businesses looking to improve their marketing effectiveness and scale their content creation efforts.

Facilitating Education or Training

The chatbot can generate study materials, provide feedback on writing assignments, and even help with language learning. We will also look into this in more detail later on.

As you converse with the chatbot, it can deduce from your text what type of information you require, and if it cannot, it will provide you with options to help it narrow down exactly what you require. Many students or learners will benefit from this, especially if they are studying through remote systems and have no one to help them with any information, resources, or materials they may require.

For example, if you needed to write a paper on Shakespeare but didn't have any relevant material on him and didn't have much time to surf the web, you could simply type in the information you needed about the writer and it would be provided to you in a matter of seconds.

Creating a Virtual Assistant

As previously stated, the chatbot can be used as a virtual assistant that can assist its users with a variety of tasks. This can include scheduling appointments, managing emails, and providing customer service.

This is accomplished through integration with existing software tools and platforms. For example, Bing has merged with ChatGPT so that it can streamline workflow and improve productivity. The search engine is now able to function as the chatbot does, giving you relevant information and direct answers to your questions. This method is useful for businesses that want to improve operational efficiency while also providing a better user experience. These companies will save time, effort, and money as a result—not forgetting how sales and customer reach will improve.

From all of the mentioned information, you now have a better understanding of ChatGPT's history, what it can do, and how it can benefit you as an individual and your company or business. The main takeaway is that this chatbot has received a lot of attention because of its impressive language capabilities and potential applications in a variety of industries. These include healthcare, finance, and customer service. This language model works by processing input text and producing understandable and meaningful output text. ChatGPT can identify patterns and relationships in the information it receives and respond with contextually relevant and accurate information using the steps of natural language processing, machine learning, and deep learning. Overall, it is an effective tool for improving human-computer interaction and enabling new artificial intelligence applications.

However, as with any advanced technology, there are concerns about its potential impact on society, as well as the need for ethical and responsible development and applications. How will it affect the future generations? Can those who use technology for malicious purposes take advantage of such an incredible chatbot? Then again, will this AI eliminate the human workforce?

Despite all of this, we have seen how OpenAI as an organization are constantly improving their language model systems so that they can help rather than replace the human workforce. The chatbot will be beneficial as long as we use it to benefit ourselves and others. ChatGPT cannot do everything and this means that it cannot eradicate the entire human workforce.

It's time to move on to the next chapter, which discusses how the chatbot can help your business. ChatGPT has numerous advantages that will assist companies in improving their image, streamlining their functions, providing better customer support, and more. This chatbot is an excellent resource for content, copywriting, and virtual assistance. When used correctly, it can improve your business dramatically.

Chapter 3
ChatGPT for Business

Opus Research conducted a study that discovered that consumers are becoming more accepting of chatbots (Wafeq, 2023). According to the study, nearly half of the consumers polled had no preference for whether they received customer service assistance from a human or a chatbot. This shows a very large difference from what was once preferred. Customers previously wanted to interact with human agents instead of artificial intelligences for all of their customer service-related enquiries.

Businesses stand to benefit from this new change in consumer preferences. With consumer acceptance of chatbots growing, businesses that implement ChatGPT can gain a competitive advantage by providing efficient and effective customer service. The Opus Research study highlights the potential benefits of having the chatbot respond to customer queries. The service is done quickly and accurately, reducing wait times and increasing overall customer satisfaction. ChatGPT's ability to handle multiple inquiries at the same time can also improve operational efficiency and lower costs for businesses.

The same study even found that "35% of consumers want to see more businesses use chatbots" (Wafeq, 2023). This suggests that consumers are increasingly open to using chatbots to communicate with businesses, and that there is a growing demand for chatbot use in customer service.

Now that we know that the human population is moving toward getting artificial intelligence to help businesses and companies assist their customers, let's have a look at the ways in which chat-based AI, such as ChatGPT, can help your business thrive in today's market. (Schmid, 2022). What does it do, and how does it do it?

Business Use Cases for ChatGPT

As mentioned previously, the chatbot is an artificial intelligence-powered language model that can be used to automate routine tasks in a variety of fields. It can understand and generate human-like responses to a wide range of queries and requests by utilizing natural language processing and machine learning algorithms.

Compiling and Conducting Market Research

The chatbot can be used to conduct market research for your business. It can automatically monitor and analyze market trends like new products, competitors, and industry developments. It can then generate reports or alerts based on predefined criteria or research questions.

This is mainly accomplished by reading and summarizing a large number of articles: ChatGPT can collect and analyze data from a variety of sources, including surveys and online reviews. It will then provide insights into key themes and recommend new sources to investigate.

A company looking to develop a new product, for example, could use ChatGPT to investigate existing research on similar products, analyze customer reviews, and identify trends and insights about customers and the market. Businesses can save time and ensure they have the most up-to-date information at their fingertips by automating the research process, allowing them to make more informed decisions.

Brainstorming and Drafting Marketing Content

The chatbot can help with marketing content creation by suggesting headlines, writing copy for emails and advertisements, and creating social media posts. For example, a company might use it to generate a copy for an email product launch or to create a series of social media posts promoting a sale.

The chatbot can help by coming up with ideas for new products or services, marketing campaigns, and so on. For example, a company could use it to ask open-ended questions to employees, such as "What new features could we add to our product X?" It can help businesses explore new possibilities and uncover insights they might have missed otherwise.

Writing Computer Code

By generating code snippets and learning from existing coding and programming best practices, chat-based AI can help software developers save time and avoid errors. It can aid in the completion of repetitive coding tasks. A developer, for example, might use it to complete a routine task like text formatting. This enables them to focus on more complex coding challenges instead.

Automating Sales

A chatbot can assist in the automation of parts of the sales process. A company could use it to answer frequently asked questions and handle routine customer inquiries. They could also use it to generate personalized product recommendations based on a customer's previous purchases. AI can understand a customer's preferences and what they might need by using natural language processing and machine learning, making it easier to provide a more tailored experience. Automation will be covered in depth later in this chapter.

Following Up After Customers Buy Products

AI can help with after-sales support by answering frequently asked questions or directing customers to relevant resources. For example, a company may use ChatGPT to provide troubleshooting tips for a product or to suggest ways to get the most out of a service. Businesses can provide faster and more consistent support to their customers by automating these tasks, which will result in increased loyalty and satisfaction.

Providing Customized Instructions

Furthermore, the AI can generate specialized product or service instructions. Customers benefit from this by getting the most out of their purchases. A company, for example, could use

ChatGPT to provide step-by-step instructions for assembling a product or navigating a software application. As mentioned, AI can understand customer needs and preferences through machine learning and natural language processing. This can make it easier to provide clear and effective guidance.

Translating Text From One Language to Another

ChatGPT can assist businesses in communicating with customers or partners who speak different languages by translating text in real time. It can provide accurate translations quickly and efficiently by utilizing natural language processing and machine learning, allowing businesses to overcome language barriers and expand their reach.

Smoothing Out the Customer Onboarding Process

AI can assist customers with the onboarding process by answering questions and providing assistance as needed. Businesses can provide a more seamless onboarding experience while reducing churn and increasing customer satisfaction by automating these tasks.

Increasing Customer Engagement

AI can be used to personalize customer communication, provide relevant content, and respond to inquiries in real time. As mentioned previously, by using natural language processing and machine learning, it can understand customer needs and preferences. This makes it easier to build stronger relationships and increase customer loyalty (and therefore retention) over time.

ChatGPT and Automation of Routine Tasks

One of ChatGPT's key advantages is its ability to increase productivity by automating time-consuming and repetitive tasks (Sanchez, 2022). It can, for example, be used to

- schedule and organize meetings
- manage tasks and project timelines
- provide performance updates
- coordinate with team members
- identify and prioritize product development
- manage product releases
- process orders and returns
- provide product information and documentation
- provide technical support
- monitor and analyze market trends
- monitor social media
- track and analyze customer data
- send targeted marketing campaigns

It can free up time and resources by automating these tasks, allowing you to focus on more important and complex tasks like strategic planning and decision-making. It can also improve response accuracy and consistency, shorten response times, and provide customers with 24/7 support.

Overall, it can improve productivity, accuracy, and consistency of responses by automating routine tasks across multiple fields using natural language processing and machine learning algorithms.

What Automation Can ChatGPT Handle?

If you were wondering about what kind of automation the chatbot can handle, let's take a detailed look into this now. The chatbot can assist your business with more than one type of automation service. Isn't this great news?

Streamlining and Enhancing Processes Using Automation

AI can assist in the automation of routine tasks such as data entry and task and appointment scheduling. This frees up employees' time to concentrate on more strategic tasks.

Scheduling and Organizing Meetings

A company, for example, could use ChatGPT to schedule meetings automatically. The chatbot can schedule and organize meetings based on predefined rules and preferences by checking calendars, sending invites and reminders, and updating schedules. It can also help with team coordination by sharing files or information based on predefined workflows.

Managing Tasks and Project Timelines

The chatbot can be used to manage project timelines and tasks by assigning tasks, tracking progress, and generating reports or notifications for milestones and deadlines.

Providing Performance Updates

It can generate reports or dashboards that summarize key metrics and KPIs such as revenue, customer satisfaction, and engagement to provide performance updates.

Managing Emails

It can be used to manage and organize email messages, such as by subject or sender.

Automating Product Development and Support

The chatbot can help a business at all levels of the product development process.

Identifying and Prioritizing Product Development

By analyzing data and making recommendations, ChatGPT can help product managers identify customer needs, analyze market trends, and prioritize product development efforts.

Managing Product Releases

It can assist in the management of product releases by coordinating tasks, tracking progress, notifying stakeholders, and generating release notes or documentation.

Providing Product Demos

It can generate interactive and personalized demos that highlight product features and benefits based on customer preferences or use cases to provide product demos.

Managing Product Information and Documentation

It can be used to provide product information to customers quickly and easily by organizing, updating, and distributing product documentation such as user guides, user manuals, and FAQs.

Answering Customer Questions

Company chatbots powered by ChatGPT can handle basic customer inquiries and support requests. The chatbot is able to respond to customer questions by generating personalized responses based on customer queries, preferences, or behavior. It is able to answer common questions and resolve simple issues, allowing human agents to concentrate on the more complex issues.

Processing Orders and Returns

The chatbot can help automate the order and return processes by processing customer requests, verifying information, updating databases, and generating order or return confirmations.

Providing Technical Support

The chatbot can respond to commonly-asked customer questions about a product or service, such as its features, specifications, pricing, and availability, by using predefined responses or accessing relevant databases. ChatGPT can also assist with troubleshooting common problems. It can offer technical assistance by answering common technical questions and escalating more complex issues to human agents.

Automating Market Research and Analysis

AI can be used to automate data entry tasks like processing and analyzing large amounts of data from multiple sources. Needless to say, this can benefit your business greatly.

Generating Leads

The chatbot can be used to automatically collect and analyze customer data (such as behaviors, demographics, and interests) from a variety of sources, including social media and online directories, in order to identify potential sales leads. After it identifies patterns, trends, and insights, ChatGPT can then generate recommendations or alerts for potential opportunities that can be used to inform business decisions.

ChatGPT is also useful for updating customer records based on email correspondence. Businesses can improve efficiency, reduce errors, and boost overall productivity by automating these tasks.

Gathering Customer Feedback

ChatGPT can also gather customer feedback more directly. Based on predefined criteria or research questions, the chatbot can create surveys, collect and analyze responses, and generate reports or insight based on that information.

Monitoring Social Media

ChatGPT can monitor and analyze social media activity in order to identify trends and opportunities. It can do this by searching for mentions of a company or its products and tracking sentiments. The chatbot can then generate reports or alerts for business insights or issues that may need to be addressed.

Sending Targeted Marketing Campaigns

It can send personalized marketing campaigns based on customer behavior, preferences, or feedback by analyzing customer data and generating personalized messages or recommendations.

Automating Content Creation

ChatGPT can be used to generate content, such as social media posts and blog articles, based on input from businesses and their target audiences. It can create content that is both persuasive and on-brand by utilizing natural language processing and machine learning. This saves time while also improving marketing results.

In conclusion, ChatGPT can significantly boost productivity by automating routine tasks in a variety of fields such as product management, customer support, marketing, and sales. As technology advances, we can expect to see even more applications and benefits from ChatGPT and other AI-powered automation tools.

Before you can use the benefits that come from ChatGPT in business, you will need to integrate the ChatGPT system with your company or business platform or website. The way to do this is by using plugins. We will look into plugins in further detail in Chapter 8, but for now let's move on to using prompt engineering.

Using Prompt Engineering

The process of designing and creating prompts for conversational AI models such as ChatGPT is referred to as prompt engineering. A prompt is a message or question that starts a conversation with an artificial intelligence system. Prompt engineering is used in business to create chatbots, virtual assistants, and other conversational interfaces that can interact with customers, answer questions, and provide support.

What Are Prompts?

Prompts are messages or questions that a user presents to an AI system to start a conversation or gather information. Prompts can be simple or complex, and they are intended to help the user navigate a conversation or transaction.

Before we move on to formulating good prompts, let's first look at the difference between prompts that can be used with ChatGPT and prompts that are used to streamline business. The difference between these prompts is that conversational prompts are more casual or have general context in them. You can use them to start a discussion or even ask a question. They are open-ended. For example, "Tell me about the history of the evolution of human beings."

On the other hand, a streamlined business prompt is more specific and has a specific goal for the purpose of the interaction. Basically, these prompts are related to getting specific information, helping with some business-related processes, and completing specific tasks. These prompts are focused on goals.

An example includes, "Get me the financial sales report for the last year."

How to Formulate a Good Prompt

A good prompt should be clear, concise, and relevant to the user's needs. Here are some pointers on how to create a good prompt:

- **Be Specific:** Use clear and specific language to describe what the user must do or provide.
- **Be Concise:** Make your prompts brief and to the point. Long prompts can be perplexing and may discourage users from participating.
- **Be Relevant:** Make certain that your prompts are pertinent to the user's needs and the context of the conversation.
- **Use Natural Language:** Write your prompts in a natural, easy-to-understand conversational tone.

Prompt Types and How to Improve Them If They Produce Poor Results

In conversational AI systems, various types of prompts, such as open-ended prompts, multiple-choice prompts, and yes/no prompts, can be used. There are several ways to improve a prompt that produces poor results. Here are a few pointers:

- **Use More Specific Language:** If a prompt is too broad, the results may be inaccurate. Use more specific language that is tailored to the user's requirements.
- **Use More Examples:** If a prompt does not yield accurate results, it is possible that the system requires more examples of how to respond to that prompt.
- **Test and Adjust:** Test various versions of the prompt and make changes based on the results. Continue to fine-tune the prompt until it produces accurate results.

Examples of Good and Bad Prompts For Business

Let's take a look at an example of a good prompt and an example of a bad prompt (Yalalov, 2022).

"What is your preferred method of payment?" is a good prompt example.

"What do you want to do now?" is a bad prompt example.

The first prompt is straightforward, specific, and pertinent to the user's requirements. The second prompt is too vague. It also does not provide any direction for the user.

There are three ways to improve your prompts so that the AI can understand just what exactly you need and give you the required content. Let's have a look at these three levels to implement to your prompt writing.

Ways to Improve Prompts

Level 1: Beginner

The beginner level improves prompts by understanding the fundamental principles of prompt engineering. Defining the objectives, gathering training data, and designing the prompts are all part of this process.

Level 2: Context

The second level entails providing context for the prompts, which means comprehending the customer's requirements, the context of the conversation, and the possible responses to the prompts.

Level 3: Roleplaying Context and Proofreading

The third level entails roleplaying scenarios and proofreading the prompts. This entails putting the prompts to the test with real users and adjusting them based on their feedback. Proofreading the prompts also ensures that they are clear, concise, and relevant to the user's needs.

Steps to Prompt Implementation

Now that you understand how to write good prompts, let's look at an example of how you could use the chatbot in a customer service setting.

Step 1: Define the Goals

The goal is to use the chatbot to improve customer service by responding to customer inquiries in a timely and accurate manner.

Step 2: Gather Training Data

Gather customer inquiries and responses to serve as training data for the chatbot model. This data can be sourced from customer service logs, email exchanges, and other customer interactions.

Step 3: Design the Prompts

Make a list of prompts that cover common customer questions. These prompts should be written in a way that allows the model to understand and respond to them correctly.

Step 4: Train the Model

Train the chatbot model using the training data and prompts. This can be accomplished through the use of various machine learning techniques, such as transfer learning.

Step 5: Evaluate the Model

Input a set of test inquiries and evaluate the accuracy and usefulness of the responses to put the chatbot model to the test.

Step 6: Analyze the Results

Analyze the evaluation results to identify areas where the model could be improved. This can include identifying common customer inquiries that the model is unable to respond accurately to.

Step 7: Refine the Model

Use the results of the analysis to improve the language model by adding more training data, changing the prompts, or changing the training procedure. This will help the model's responses to customer inquiries become more accurate and helpful over time.

Example Prompts for Business

Now that you have seen how to implement prompts for ChatGPT for your business-related uses, here are some examples of business-related prompts, as well as explanations of how to use them:

- **"Can you generate a list of potential customers for our new product?"**

Businesses that are launching a new product and need assistance identifying potential customers can use this prompt. The AI can use a variety of sources, such as demographic data, online behavior, and past purchase history, to generate a list of potential customers for the company's marketing campaigns.

- **"What are the top keywords related to our industry?"**

Businesses can gain a better understanding of the keywords that are most relevant to their industry by requesting this prompt. This information can be used to improve their online visibility by optimizing their website and content for search engines.

- **"What are some strategies we can use to improve customer retention?"**

This prompt can be useful for businesses looking for ways to improve customer retention. Based on data analysis, AI can make suggestions such as offering loyalty programs, providing excellent customer service, and sending personalized communications to customers.

- **"What are the key trends in our industry that we should be aware of?"**

Businesses can stay current on industry trends and developments by asking this prompt. This data can be used to inform business strategy and make informed decisions about investments and new product development.

- **"Can you help us optimize our supply chain?"**

Businesses that want to improve the efficiency of their supply chain can use this prompt. Data such as supplier performance, inventory levels, and transportation costs can be analyzed by AI to suggest ways to optimize the supply chain and reduce costs.

Overall, these prompts show how artificial intelligence can be used to support business operations and decision-making, resulting in increased efficiency, profitability, and growth.

Here Come the Questions…

According to one of the recent articles (CBS News, 2021), many questions have come about. These may be troubling to those who have only begun looking into AI. But worry not: Like with every other situation that we experience daily, there is always some negativity and questioning that puts a little bit of doubt into things we like, are learning about, or are even starting to find out about.

Let's look at the current trending questions and myths swimming around AI today.

Will ChatGPT Replace Jobs?

The answer is not simple because it is dependent on the type of job and the level of automation that AI and machine learning can achieve. While some jobs may be challenged by automation, there are still many that require human skills and expertise. It is important to note, however, that AI and machine learning are still in their infancy, and it is difficult to predict their long-term impact on the job market (Ahmed, 2023).

List of Jobs With Risk of Replacements

Let's have a look at some of the jobs that may be threatened by AI and machine learning, which include:

- **Content creation:** ChatGPT and other AI models can generate human-like text, potentially reducing the need for human writers in some situations. If we have AI that is capable of doing all sorts of content creation, then eventually there will be less demand for writers. The main reason why this would occur is because AI like ChatGPT shows that it can come up with content much more quickly and easily than a human being would.
- **Data entry:** By recognizing and processing data from various sources, AI can automate data entry tasks. This will reduce the need for a human workforce, as AI will be much more accurate and faster.
- **Customer service:** Chatbots and other AI-powered tools can handle basic customer service inquiries, reducing the need for human representatives.
- **Transcription and translation:** In some cases, artificial intelligence can transcribe and translate audio and text faster and more accurately than humans. Here human beings may not be eliminated as there may be some inaccuracies that may occur when an AI has to translate and transcribe certain text. So AI will be used to a certain extent but it will be monitored by a human being, as there can be grammatical errors and information which might not be true.

- **Routine administrative tasks:** AI can automate administrative tasks like scheduling and email management. This will eliminate the human workforce as it saves time, effort, and money.

From this information, we can see that AI will not be able to eliminate the entire workforce. There are certain jobs that it can do, and it does them perfectly. However, there are certain things that only a human being is capable of doing. If we had to give everything up to an AI, there would be many errors and blind spots that it would miss. Remember that AI is accurate but it is not omnipotent.

We will look at the limitations of AI in one of the latter chapters. But for now we know that it is perfect at what it is programmed to do. Also, it is adapting and learning every day. But this does not mean that it will eliminate the human workforce. There is no need to fear that you will lose your job to a robot in the near future. However, it is vital that we also learn to improve. If we remain in one position for too long, stagnant, there will always be someone much more accomplished and more knowledgeable who will eventually pop up and replace us. Similar to this situation, AI is also learning and improving every day. It will always get better than it was yesterday. So, we too must learn new things and improve so that we are not left behind.

What People Can Do (Answered by ChatGPT Itself)

While some jobs may be threatened by automation, there are still many that require human skills and expertise. People can prepare for the changing job market by doing the following:

- Concentrate on developing skills that AI can not replicate, such as creativity, emotional intelligence, and critical thinking.
- Keep up with the latest technology and trends, and be open to new tools and workflows.
- Accept AI technology and learn to collaborate with AI-powered tools and systems.
- Concentrate on niche and specialized topics where human knowledge is still highly valued.
- Collaborate with AI, and use it to improve your skills and productivity.

Looking back at all of the above information, we can see that it will assist a business in many ways. The opportunities and benefits range from lead generation to research. You can decide how far you want to take this AI and how much it will help you and your business. We can see from the questions that it is not here to replace the human workforce. Its main purpose is to assist the human workforce in every way possible.

The best way to get the most out of this chatbot is to use the right prompts and questions. Remember that we can ask any type of question and receive any type of answer. Only when the chatbot understands what you're saying will you be shown the appropriate content. It is very important to train it first by providing relevant information. You can then ask an open-ended or closed question, and the chatbot will interpret it as best it can based on the information you provide. To make the most of it, make your prompt brief, clear, and to-the-point. After all, there should be no room for the imagination; the chatbot will not be able to generate content out of thin air. The bottom line is that the chatbot has limitless potential to help your business. However, the road will only go as far as you can take it.

Do note that when it comes to ChatGPT and business, you can integrate with Slack. This will make your virtual office so much easier to handle. To do this, you must create a custom Slack app that will connect to ChatGPT. The benefit will include your users interacting with the AI through direct messages and dedicated channels. This will allow them to get immediate responses and support within their virtual workspace.

Now that you know how to make use of prompts, it's time to move on to the next chapter, which discusses ChatGPT and the advantages it can provide you as a business owner in terms of customer service. We examine how it can assist you as well as the benefits it can provide to you and to your customers. Let's get started.

Chapter 4
ChatGPT for Customer Service

Conversational banking has grown in popularity as a way for banks to interact with their customers in recent years. One way banks are leveraging conversational banking is by improving customer service with AI-powered chatbots such as ChatGPT. The case study from UXDA (Alex et al, n.d.) is a great example of this, as it details how one bank was able to significantly improve their customer experience by implementing it.

The bank in question, according to the case study, was struggling to keep up with the high volume of customer inquiries and support requests it was receiving. This resulted in long wait times, dissatisfied customers, and a negative impact on the bank's reputation. To address these concerns, the bank enlisted the help of ChatGPT to enhance its conversational banking capabilities.

The bank was able to provide personalized and accurate responses to their customers' inquiries by using ChatGPT, significantly reducing wait times and improving customer satisfaction. It was also able to provide customers with real-time access to their account information, transaction history, and other important banking details, further improving the customer experience.

Overall, the case study shows how AI-powered chatbots like ChatGPT have the potential to transform the banking industry by providing more efficient and effective customer service experiences.

Customer Service

Chatbots can be used for customer service in a variety of ways by businesses. The benefits are endless due to the AI handling these tasks for you. You could even use a customer service chatbot for most of these use cases (Staff, 2023).

How to Integrate With a Chatbot

First, you will have to develop a chatbot. You can do this by using a platform like Dialogflow or IBM Watson Assistant. Once the chatbot is done, you can integrate ChatGPT as the backend for generating responses for your chatbot. As soon as this is done, your customers can get the support they need as well as communicate much more easily.

How ChatGPT Can Help Businesses Improve Their Customer Service

Let's go into detail about how AI can help your business improve your customer service. There are many methods and most of them are easy to integrate into your company platform. If you aren't a software or technical person, don't fret, because you can eventually get someone to do these integrations for you. Do note that we will go over these integrations in Chapter 8, but for now let's just look at what it can offer your business.

- **Automation:** As mentioned in the previous chapter, ChatGPT can automate many aspects of customer service, including answering frequently asked questions, routing inquiries to the appropriate department, and scheduling appointments. This allows human customer service representatives to handle more complex issues. A retail store, for example, can use it to answer frequently asked questions about store hours, return policies, delivery details, processing returns, and product availability.
- **24/7 availability:** ChatGPT can provide uninterrupted customer service 24 hours a day, 7 days a week. This is especially beneficial for businesses that operate across time zones or have customers in different parts of the world. A software company, for example, can use it to provide round-the-clock technical support to its customers.
- **Consistency:** It can provide consistent responses to customer queries, which can aid in the development of

customer trust and credibility. This is especially important for companies that have multiple customer service representatives who may give different answers to the same question. A financial services company, for example, can use the chatbot to ensure that its customers receive consistent and accurate information about its services.

- **Scalability:** It can handle an unlimited number of customer inquiries at the same time, allowing businesses to scale their customer service operations without hiring more agents. A healthcare provider, for example, can use it to handle a high volume of patient inquiries regarding appointment scheduling, prescription refills, and medical billing.
- **Summarization:** It can generate summaries of customer and agent conversations, which can be useful for agents who need to review previous interactions with customers quickly. For example, an insurance company can use it to provide summaries of customer claims and inquiries to its claims adjusters.
- **Translation:** ChatGPT can provide real-time translations of customer inquiries and responses, which is useful for businesses that serve customers who speak multiple languages. For example, a travel company can use it to provide international customers with customer service in multiple languages.

Overall, it provides several advantages to businesses looking to improve their customer service operations. It is capable of automating routine tasks, providing consistent and accurate information, and scaling operations to handle a high volume of inquiries. It can also provide conversation summaries and translations to help businesses serve customers more effectively.

Prompt Ideas for Customer Service

As previously stated, you must use prompts that will provide the best response from the AI. Your question should be brief and easy to understand. It should also leave no room for speculation. Let's take a look at some of the prompt ideas you could use or create similar ones for your business (Objartel, 2023).

Categorizing and Prioritizing

- "Use a ticketing system to categorize and prioritize customer inquiries based on their urgency and complexity."
- "Develop a system for flagging and escalating high-priority issues to ensure they receive prompt attention."
- "Analyze customer data and feedback to identify common issues and prioritize them for resolution."

Sending Issue Notifications

- "Send timely and informative notifications to customers affected by an issue."
- "Provide updates on the progress of resolving the issue."
- "Offer tips or workarounds to minimize the impact of the issue."

Troubleshooting

- "Ask the customer specific questions to identify the root cause of the problem."
- "Offer step-by-step instructions or visual aids to guide the customer through the troubleshooting process."
- "Suggest alternative solutions if the initial troubleshooting steps do not work."

Replying to Customer Complaints

- "Apologize for the issue X and offer a solution or compensation."
- "Express empathy and understanding of the customer's frustration."
- "Provide clear and concise information about the next steps to resolve the issue."

Replying to Customer Reviews

- "Thank the customer for taking the time to leave a review."
- "Acknowledge any positive feedback and address any negative feedback."
- "Offer solutions or suggestions for improvement based on the customer's feedback."

Driving Engagement With the Company's Offers

- "Highlight the benefits and features of the company's offers to the customer."
- "Personalize the offer by tailoring it to the customer's needs and preferences."
- "Provide additional resources or support to help the customer take advantage of the offer."

Generating Content for Customers and Prospects

- "Create educational resources such as guides, tutorials, or webinars to help customers and prospects learn about the company's products or services."
- "Develop engaging social media posts or email campaigns to keep customers and prospects informed about the company's latest news and updates."
- "Collaborate with the marketing team to create compelling content that resonates with the target audience."

Repurposing Knowledge Base Articles

- "Repurpose existing knowledge base articles into other formats such as videos, infographics, or podcasts to reach a wider audience."
- "Update and republish outdated or underperforming knowledge base articles to improve their relevance and effectiveness."

- "Use customer feedback and search data to identify gaps in the knowledge base and develop new articles to address those gaps."

Monitoring Quality

- "Conduct regular quality assurance checks to ensure that agents are meeting performance standards."
- "Use customer feedback and metrics to identify areas for improvement and implement training or coaching programs."
- "Continuously review and refine customer service processes and procedures to ensure they are effective and efficient."

Coding Automated Tasks

- "Automate routine tasks such as data entry, appointment scheduling, or order processing to free up agents' time for more complex issues."
- "Use machine learning algorithms to automate responses to common customer inquiries."
- "Develop chatbots or other AI-powered tools to handle simple customer service requests and provide customers with 24/7 support."

Helping New Agents Adapt Their Tone of Voice

- "Provide new agents with examples of positive and negative tones of voice in customer service interactions."
- "Offer training and coaching on how to adjust the tone of voice based on the customer's emotional state or the nature of the issue."
- "Encourage agents to seek feedback and guidance from more experienced team members to help them improve their tone of voice."

Acting as a Proxy for Customer Chats to Test Agents

- "Act as a 'mystery shopper' to test the quality and effectiveness of customer service interactions."
- "Provide agents with feedback and coaching based on the results of the testing."
- "Use the data and metrics from the testing to identify areas for improvement in the customer service process."

Providing Examples for Training Soft Skills

- "Provide examples of effective communication, active listening, and empathy in customer service interactions."
- "Develop scenarios or role-playing exercises to help agents practice and improve their soft skills."

- "Use customer feedback and agent performance metrics to identify areas where additional training or coaching may be needed."

Problems and Limitations for Customer Service

Despite the fact that any business can use AI to handle the majority of their customer service-related automation and answering, there are a few limitations and issues to be aware of. Let's take a closer look at each of them.

Limitations

- **Limited capabilities:** Chatbots and other automated systems can only handle a limited number of tasks and questions and are not as adaptable as human agents. A chatbot, for example, may be incapable of handling complex technical support issues or providing emotional support to upset customers.
- **Lack of personalization:** Automated systems may be unable to tailor responses to the needs and preferences of individual customers. A chatbot, for example, may be unable to recall a customer's previous interactions with the company or their personal information.
- **Potential for errors:** Automated systems may make errors due to a lack of understanding of the customer's question or technical glitches. A chatbot, for example, may give a customer incorrect information or fail to understand a customer's request.

Potential Problems and Solutions

Now that you've seen the limitations of the chatbot, it's time to move on to the potential problems you could experience.

Problem A: Outdated Information

Chatbots may have access to a large amount of information, but they may not be up to date or complete in their knowledge. A chatbot, for example, may provide out-of-date information about a product's features or pricing.

Solution

Companies should make certain that their chatbots have access to the most up-to-date and accurate information. This problem can be mitigated with regular updates and maintenance.

Problem B: Authentic Appearance, Incorrect Information

While automated systems can be programmed to sound like human agents, they can also provide inaccurate or misleading information. A chatbot, for example, may incorrectly inform a customer that a product is in stock when it is actually out of stock.

Solution

Companies should provide guidelines and training to ensure that their chatbots provide customers with true and accurate information. They may also include disclaimers to inform customers that they are interacting with a chatbot.

Problem C: High Computational Effort

Chatbots and other automated systems require a significant amount of computational power and resources to function properly. This can be difficult for businesses with limited resources.

Solution

Companies can reduce computational costs by optimizing their use of language models and other AI technologies. They might also think about outsourcing customer service to third-party providers who have the resources and expertise to manage automated systems.

Problem D: Action Limitations

Chatbots may be limited in the tasks they can perform and may be unable to handle complex or specialized requests. A chatbot, for example, may be unable to assist a customer with a specific technical issue.

Solution

Companies should train their chatbots to handle specific support tasks and provide a clear path for customers to escalate their requests to human agents as needed. This can help ensure that customers receive the assistance they require, even if the chatbot is unable to provide it.

Overall, we have seen the many benefits of having the chatbot assist your business with customer-related services. From automation and 24/7 availability to summaries and translations, the opportunities are enormous. Not only does it save you time, but it also helps save you money. The bottom line is that if your customers are satisfied, sales and word-of-mouth advertising will go up. After all, everyone wants to bank with or buy from a company that values its clients and saves them time and money.

Despite the great advantages of AI, it is also important that you understand the limitations and problems that you may experience when using it. There are solutions you could come up with in order to make do with AI without experiencing any of the problems or limitations.

Now that we have looked at all of the above information and know how to use the correct prompts to assist with customer-related services as well, let's move on to how ChatGPT can assist with marketing for your business.

Chapter 5
ChatGPT for Marketing and Sales

As the use of AI in the workplace grows, businesses are discovering new ways to leverage this technology to reach more customers than ever before. According to a recent Fishbowl survey (Fishbowl Insights, 2022), nearly 30% of professionals in the United States have already used the chatbot or other AI tools for work-related tasks. This is especially true for marketing and advertising workers, with 37% reporting use of AI, closely followed by those in technology and consulting.

In this chapter, we will look at how businesses can use the chatbot to reach out to more customers and improve their customer service efforts. We'll go over the advantages of using it, best practices for implementing this technology, and real-world examples of businesses that have successfully used this AI to improve their customer experience. Whether you're a small business owner or a marketing professional, this chapter will give you valuable insights into how it can help you grow your customer base and improve your bottom line.

Using ChatGPT Across All Sales Funnel Stages

The best way to use the AI when it comes to sales funnel stages is to integrate it with your website or landing page. Once this is done, it will help with personalized recommendations, checking out, and even answering questions. This will improve your user experience and boost sales.

To do this, you can integrate it with certain platforms like Google Docs or your company's content management system (CMS). This will help to streamline the content creation process for business (Staff, 2023).

Content Creation Using ChatGPT

When it comes to content creation and lead generation, you can use the AI to come up with posts, captions, newsletters, and more. It can help at all stages of the process.

Use Cases

Idea Brainstorming

ChatGPT can assist you in developing new and unique content ideas. For example, if you're making a video series about "productivity tips," it can suggest new and exciting concepts for each video.

Outlines

The chatbot can generate a blog post or article outline, including suggested headings and subheadings. It, for example, can provide an outline that includes sections such as "Benefits of Healthy Living," "Healthy Eating Tips," and "Exercise and Fitness" if you're writing about "healthy living."

Title Suggestions

It can help you come up with catchy titles for your content. For example, if you were writing a blog post about "digital marketing," ChatGPT could suggest titles like "10 Digital Marketing Strategies for Small Businesses" or "The Ultimate Guide to Digital Marketing in 2023."

Captions for Videos

The chatbot can generate accurate and interesting captions for your videos. For example, if you're making a video about "productivity tips," it can generate captions that highlight the key points and are search-engine optimized.

Scripts for Videos and Podcasts

Likewise, it can assist you in developing engaging and informative video scripts. For example, if you're making a video about "digital marketing," it can assist you in developing a script that's well-researched, engaging, and informative. The AI can also help you write interesting podcast scripts. For example, an influencer could use ChatGPT to create engaging content for the next podcast episode based on their brand.

Research and Writing

The chatbot can assist you in conducting research on a particular topic and then creating content based on that research. For instance, if you're writing an article about "the benefits of mindfulness," it can assist you in locating relevant studies and then writing content based on those studies.

Blog Posts

It can also create complete blog posts from scratch based on the topic and keywords you provide. The chatbot, for example, can generate a complete blog post with well-researched content and sources if you're writing a blog post about "digital transformation."

Editing

The chatbot can assist you with grammar, spelling, and tone editing. For example, if you're creating an email newsletter, it can review the content and make suggestions to improve readability and engagement.

Summarizing Extensive Content

It can assist in the condensing of long-form content, such as white papers or e-books, into smaller lead magnets, such as a one-page summary or infographic.

Inbound Lead Generation

ChatGPT can assist you with inbound lead generation activities, such as content creation, webinars and live events, and referral programs. It, for example, can be used to generate topics for blog posts, video scripts for webinars, and copy for referral program landing pages. Essentially, it can generate lead-generating content, such as a blog post that offers tips and tricks for optimizing website traffic.

SEO Keywords and Optimization

Assume you're a marketer looking to generate leads for a new product launch. The chatbot can generate a list of relevant keywords and phrases for a given topic. For example, if you're writing about "healthy meal prep," it can suggest related keywords like "meal prep recipes," "healthy eating," and "food prep tips." This can be used to raise awareness of your brand.

Developing content that focuses on specific SEO keywords is one way to attract potential leads to your website. ChatGPT, for example, can recommend long-tail keywords that are popular in a specific industry or location. It can create SEO-friendly blog post topics, ad copy, and email subject lines such as "best CRM software for small businesses" or "top New York City real estate agents" to help you reach your target audience.

Use Cases

- **Calls to action and lead magnets:** The chatbot can assist in the creation of lead-generating ad copy, such as "Get a free consultation today" or "Limited time offer: 50% off all services." There are plenty of ways to create compelling calls to action and lead magnets to entice website visitors to share their contact information with you.
- **Forms and surveys:** You can use ChatGPT to create forms and surveys that will help you better understand your audience and their needs. It can create forms that

are optimized for lead generation, such as a contact form with fields for name, email, and phone number.

- **Quizzes:** Likewise, it can help you create quizzes that engage website visitors while also collecting their contact information, such as "Take our quiz and find out what type of entrepreneur you are."
- **Giveaways:** It can be used to promote lead generation giveaways such as "Enter our giveaway and win a free consultation with one of our experts."
- **Live events:** "Join us at our next event and get a free consultation with one of our experts," for example, could be used to promote live events and generate leads using the chatbot.
- **Webinars:** ChatGPT can assist in the creation of lead-generating webinar content, such as "Join our free webinar and learn how to grow your business with social media."
- **Referrals:** It can assist in the development of referral programs that encourage current customers to refer their friends and family.

Outbound Lead Generation

Outbound lead generation activities such as social selling, personal branding, database cleaning, and list management can also be assisted by ChatGPT. It can be used to generate templates for cold email campaigns, LinkedIn messages for outreach, cold call scripts, and more.

Use Cases

- **Ad retargeting:** ChatGPT can be used to create ad copy that is intended to retarget leads who have previously expressed interest in a product or service.
- **Database cleaning and list management:** It can assist in automating the process of updating and cleaning email lists to ensure that sales teams are reaching out to the right people. It, for example, can analyze email addresses and recommend which ones are likely to be outdated or invalid.
- **Topic research and campaign ideas for newsletter content:** ChatGPT can assist you in researching topics for your email newsletters and campaigns by generating relevant and engaging ideas. It, for example, can suggest product-related topics to include in your newsletters, such as gift guides, product reviews, and special offers, if you run an e-commerce store.
- **Email Marketing With ChatGPT:** It can help with the development of effective email campaigns that encourage lead generation, such as "10% off your first purchase" or "Join our VIP program for exclusive offers and discounts."

The Significance of ChatGPT in an Email Campaign

This is another area in which ChatGPT really shines. Using ChatGPT in email marketing can improve the personalization, relevance, and engagement of your campaigns. You can create customized email content that resonates with your target audience and drives better results by leveraging the power of language generation (Staff, 2023). Here are some of the major benefits:

- **Automation:** it can automate many aspects of your email marketing campaigns, including content creation, segmentation, and optimization, saving you time and money.
- **Enhanced participation:** The AI can assist sales teams in crafting personalized and compelling cold emails that are more likely to elicit responses. It, for example, can recommend specific and effective subject lines, opening sentences, or email body content based on a company's industry and target audience. ChatGPT-generated personalized and relevant emails can increase open and click-through rates, resulting in increased engagement and conversions.
- **Scalability:** It can be used to generate unlimited amounts of unique email content. This makes it ideal for large-scale email marketing campaigns.
- **Cost-effectiveness:** It can help you save money on hiring copywriters or marketing agencies by automating various email marketing tasks.

- **Language generation:** Its language generation capabilities can assist you in creating more compelling and creative email content that stands out in the inboxes of your subscribers.

Examples of ChatGPT Email Prompts

Topic Investigation for Newsletter Content and Campaign Concepts

- "Generate 10 ideas for a Mother's Day gift guide."
- "Come up with the top five Christmas celebration ideas."

Newsletter Bodies

- "Create an engaging and creative body text for a Black Friday email campaign."
- "Create exciting content for the upcoming book celebration, which will be held in London on March 22, 2024."

Email Marketing Workflow Automation

- "Construct a welcome email sequence of three personalized emails."

Email Segmentation

- "Suggest three new email list segments based on subscriber behavior."
- "Suggest three personalized email campaigns for each of our buyer personas."

Subject Line Optimization

- "Create five subject lines for an upcoming email campaign and rank them in order of potential open rate."

Email Design and Template Creation

- "Design an eye-catching email template for our monthly newsletter."

A/B Testing and Optimization

- "Create two versions of a product launch email and recommend which one would perform better based on prior data."

Now that we have had a look at ChatGPT email prompts, let's move on to writing an email prompt.

How to Write an Email Prompt

When creating an email prompt for ChatGPT, make sure to be specific and provide clear instructions. To help it generate more accurate and relevant responses, use natural language and include any relevant information or data.

Some Tips

- Begin small and test it on a few email marketing tasks before expanding it to larger campaigns.
- Analyze and monitor the performance of ChatGPT-generated content to identify areas for enhancement and optimization.
- To get the most out of the chatbot, combine it with other email marketing tools and techniques.

Despite the chatbot being so adept, there are a few limitations.

Limits of ChatGPT in Email Marketing

It is a powerful email marketing tool, but it does have limitations. This is the perfect example of just why AI is unable to compete with a human being who is able to change their style and tone of writing to suit specific needs. It may, for example, be unable to understand the context or tone of your brand, resulting in inappropriate or irrelevant content. To ensure the quality and relevance of your email marketing campaigns, ChatGPT must be used in conjunction with human input and oversight.

However, keep in mind that when you encounter limitations, it is not the end of the road, especially when it comes to AI. You can always use prompts to work around what the AI is incapable of doing. If the ChatGPT chatbot is unable to write an email copy that conveys your brand message or tone, you can provide enough information to the chatbot that it understands what you are attempting to convey and in what tone. You can also tell the chatbot what type of style you require for your email copy.

Tips and Best Practices for Sales and Lead Generation

There are various other ways the AI can assist with lead generation (IndustryTrends, 2023).

- **Sales training and feedback.** During sales calls or demos, ChatGPT can provide real-time coaching and feedback to sales teams. It, for example, can analyze the tone and content of a conversation and recommend ways to improve messaging or rapport with a potential lead.
- **Business chatbot creation.** Furthermore, you can use it to build chatbots that will assist you in engaging with potential customers and guiding them through the sales funnel.
- **Interest, decision, action, retention.** It can assist in the automation of the lead nurturing process by recommending content or messaging that is relevant to potential leads at each stage of the funnel. It, for example, can recommend blog post topics or email templates that are tailored to specific stages of the

funnel. By efficiently engaging with your leads, you increase your chances of retaining them as customers in the long term.

ChatGPT for Market Research

ChatGPT is a natural language processing (NLP) model that can be used in market research to quickly and efficiently analyze and understand large amounts of data. Let's go over some of the things to think about when conducting market research with ChatGPT (Nosewiczj, 2023):

How to Use ChatGPT for Market Research

In market research, it can be used to conduct surveys, analyze customer feedback, and generate reports. By feeding text data into the model, it can generate insights, identify trends, and make recommendations based on the data.

A market research firm, for example, can use the chatbot to analyze social media comments about a product and extract key themes and sentiments. The model can also be used to build chatbots that interact with customers while collecting data for market research.

Before we go into detail about market research, let first look at how to use the AI for this purpose with a social media listening tool. To use this, you would need to first develop a tool that uses the AI to analyze and summarize social media conversations. This will let you get access to customer preferences, insights, and new trends. This tool could then be integrated into social media platforms like Facebook and Instagram.

Why is ChatGPT Market Research Important?

It can assist businesses in streamlining their market research processes and gaining insight into the needs, preferences, and behaviors of their customers and/or target audiences. This can assist businesses in making data-driven decisions to improve their products and services while increasing customer satisfaction.

Among the benefits are the following:

- **Improving market research:** The chatbot can help with research by conducting surveys, collecting data, and analyzing the results. It can design and distribute surveys to gather information from customers and potential customers.
- **Condensing and analyzing large volumes of data:** It can condense and analyze large amounts of data efficiently, reducing the time and effort required for market research.
- **Performing competitor analysis:** It can examine competitor websites, social media platforms, and other online platforms to learn about their marketing and customer engagement strategies.
- **Generating and translating reports:** ChatGPT can generate market research data reports and summaries, making it easier for businesses to communicate insights

and recommendations. It can also translate customer reports and feedback into another language, which is useful for companies with a global presence.

- **Aiding market segmentation:** ChatGPT can help with market segmentation and understanding customer behaviors and preferences within those segments.
- **Offering customer insight:** ChatGPT provides deeper insight into customer needs, preferences, and behaviors, which can be used to improve a business's products and services.

Limitations of ChatGPT for Research

- The accuracy of the chatbot is determined by the quality of the input data.
- The model may struggle to interpret emotions accurately.
- It may not recognize cultural or regional differences in language, reducing its accuracy.

Solutions

If you're wondering how to improve the chatbot's market research capabilities, read on.

- Train it on industry-specific language and terminology.
- To gain a more comprehensive understanding of customer behavior and preferences, use ChatGPT in conjunction with other machine learning models and data analytics tools.

ChatGPT and Social Media Marketing

ChatGPT can assist salespeople and businesses in personalizing their social media posts in order to connect with potential leads more effectively. The chatbot, for example, can recommend creative captions for social media posts based on a company's target audience and industry. It is an AI-powered tool for social media marketers that can help them with content creation, community management, and campaign planning. Here are some examples of how ChatGPT can be used in social media marketing (Tanner, 2023).

How Can You Use It in Social Media Marketing?

One of the best ways to incorporate the chatbot into your brand is through social media. Let's look at how we can do this.

Ad Copy

ChatGPT can develop effective ad copy for social media marketing campaigns. It could be used by a beauty brand, for example, to create copy for Facebook ads promoting their new skincare product.

Posts on Social Media

ChatGPT facilitates the creation of lead-generating social media posts, such as "Sign up for our newsletter and receive a free ebook on social media marketing." It can generate social media posts that are tailored to specific platforms and audiences, as well as adding emojis and suggesting pictures, thus making content more engaging. Ideally, it can create viral posts in order to increase engagement and brand awareness.

For example, if you're planning a "sustainability" social media campaign, the chatbot can recommend social media posts that are optimized for each platform and will resonate with your target audience. It's critical to keep the target audience in mind when using the chatbot to generate prompts or questions for social media content. A company aimed at young adults, for example, could use it to generate prompts or questions based on popular TV shows or music festivals.

- **Facebook posts:** The chatbot can help you create interesting Facebook posts that will increase engagement and drive traffic to your website. For instance, an e-commerce store can use it to create Facebook posts promoting their most recent sale and providing a discount code to their followers.
- **LinkedIn posts:** ChatGPT can be used to assist businesses in creating engaging and informative content for LinkedIn. For example, a company could use it to create a post about the latest industry trends or news.
- **Twitter threads:** It can help you create engaging Twitter threads that can spark conversations and raise brand awareness. For instance, a technology company could use it to create a Twitter thread outlining the benefits of their most recent software update.
- **Instagram stories and Reels:** A beauty brand, for example, could use ChatGPT to create engaging

Instagram stories showcasing their latest makeup products. It could also be used by a fashion brand to create Instagram stories showcasing their latest collection and directing users to their website. Furthermore, ChatGPT can help you come up with creative and engaging ideas for Instagram Reels. A company could use it to generate ideas for a "day in the life" Reel that shows how their products are used in real life.

- **TikTok Videos:** It can be used to generate innovative and engaging TikTok video ideas. For example, a business could use the chatbot to generate ideas for a dance challenge featuring their products or to advertise their brand.
- **YouTube Videos:** Similarly, it can assist in the creation of engaging YouTube video content that can drive traffic to a website and increase brand awareness. A food brand, for instance, could use ChatGPT to create YouTube videos showcasing their recipes and directing users to their website.

Comments

It can respond to comments on social media posts, making community management easier. It, for example, can be used by an e-commerce store to respond to customer inquiries and feedback on Facebook product promotion posts.

Social Media Captions

It can help create unique and engaging captions for your social media posts. For example, a fashion brand might use it to create catchy captions for Instagram posts showcasing their latest collection.

ChatGPT can even generate captions in multiple languages, allowing brands to connect with their global audience more easily. For example, a travel company could use it to create captions in multiple languages for social media posts promoting their travel packages.

Product Promotion and Descriptions

It can create product descriptions as well as promotional content for social media posts. For instance, an electronics company could use the chatbot to generate product descriptions for social media posts promoting their latest smartphone.

Relevant Hashtags

Like keywords, ChatGPT can find relevant hashtags for your social media posts and improve the discoverability of your content. For example, a fitness influencer could use the chatbot to generate relevant hashtags for their Instagram workout routine posts.

Influencers in Your Niche

ChatGPT can assist in identifying relevant influencers in a specific niche with whom to collaborate, and crafting a message that resonates with their target audiences. (Do note that since ChatGPT only goes back to 2021, you may need to use

WebChatGPT.) A food brand, for example, could use the chatbot to find food industry influencers to promote their products on Instagram.

Content Calendars

It can help marketers plan their content strategy by creating content calendars for social media campaigns. A travel company, for example, could use it to create a content calendar for their Instagram account that highlights different travel destinations.

Overall, ChatGPT can be a valuable tool for businesses looking to streamline their social media marketing efforts and generate engaging content for their target audience. However, it is important to remember that it is not a replacement for human creativity and expertise.

To conclude, this AI chatbot ChatGPT can be used in more ways than one to promote your marketing as well as your lead generation efforts. You can use this AI to streamline and improve both market research and your social media marketing. In today's industries, more companies need to come up with social media content for their platforms. Most, if not all, people spend the majority of their free time scrolling through their social media accounts, and brands that have a social media presence that cover most of the sales out there today.

You can use this AI to improve your customers' experience by giving them personalized interactions as well as insights into your brand. You can use it to create the high-quality content that you are looking for. It would save you a lot of time to automate several of the processes that help with generating leads as well as conducting market research. This saves your company or business money and time. Your customers will be more satisfied, and sales will be boosted.

Now that you have had a look at how it can improve your business, let us move on to the next chapter, which will explore all of the possibilities that it can offer you in order to create courses. With the natural language processing capability as well as the knowledge database that the AI typically has, it has the potential to revolutionize the way that courses are delivered and made today. Just imagine what it would look like to create a course only by having a conversation with it. This upcoming chapter will give you the necessary information, as well as any resources that you would need in order to create the perfect course. You can even add a course to many existing businesses, boosting income and providing valuable information. Well, let's stop imagining and get right to it.

Chapter 6
ChatGPT for Course Creation

A course creator and entrepreneurship instructor named Rachel Lavern used ChatGPT to improve her course content by generating high-quality content and answering students' questions, according to a blog post she shared (Lavern, 2022). Specifically, she used it to build a chatbot that could answer her students' questions. The chatbot was trained on a large corpus of data related to entrepreneurship and small business management. As a result, the chatbot will be able to provide accurate and relevant answers to the students' questions.

Furthermore, it aided Rachel in the creation of course content by providing new ideas and insights on how to approach various topics. She could enter a topic and it would generate a detailed summary of the topic, complete with examples and supporting details.

Rachel's teaching experience has been greatly enhanced by the use of ChatGPT, which has allowed her to focus on more important aspects of her teaching, such as engaging students and creating hands-on activities. It also assisted her in providing a more efficient and effective learning experience for her students, as they were able to get quick and accurate answers to their questions.

In conclusion, Rachel Lavern's use of the chatbot demonstrates the technology's potential to improve course content and the teaching experience. Educators can focus on delivering high-quality instruction and engaging with their students by using a chatbot to answer students' questions and generate content ideas. The article discusses the various online content creation opportunities available to educators through the chatbot, such as creating course outlines, writing content, and scripting and editing videos. Let's look into this now.

Creating Online Courses With ChatGPT

The opportunities for using ChatGPT for course creation are endless. This artificial intelligence can help those who wish to teach provide interactive learning experiences. Now let's look at how we can use the chatbot to create courses (Ortiz, 2023).

Choosing an Effective Course Topic or Idea

You can ask ChatGPT for suggestions on profitable course topics based on your expertise or interests. "Could you recommend some profitable course topics related to marketing?" is a great example of a prompt (McDonald, 2022). You can also request that it conduct market research and competitor analysis to assist you in selecting a course topic. "Could you research and analyze market demand and competition for a web design course?" is an example of a prompt you could use.

Creating Course Content

When it comes to course content generation, you could integrate ChatGPT with your course management system or e-learning platform. This would then allow you to use the model to come up with quiz questions, create lesson plans, and more, to enhance the learning experience (Gilmore et al., 2023).

ChatGPT can be used to create online course content such as quizzes, assessments, and learning activities. Educators, for example, can use the tool to generate multiple-choice questions based on a specific topic, or to create simulations and games that engage students.

- **Ask ChatGPT to create an outline for your course based on the topic you've chosen.** It can be used to create course outlines that provide a comprehensive overview of the course, including learning objectives, topics, and assessments. Educators can enter the course topic and ChatGPT will generate a course outline complete with supporting details and examples. "Could you create an outline for a social media marketing course?" is a great example of a prompt you can use.
- **Tell ChatGPT to create content for modules.** You can request that it create content for specific modules in

your course. An example of a great prompt to try out is, "Could you create content for the first module of my photography course?"

- **Ask ChatGPT to elaborate on specific subtopics you need.** You can request that it provide more detailed explanations on specific subtopics within your course. "Could you elaborate on the concept of 'white balance' in my photography course?" is a prompt you could try for this use case.

- **Tell it to create content for course presentation.** You can request that ChatGPT create content for your course's overall presentation, such as introductions, summaries, and transitions. For example, "Could you write an introduction and summary for my cooking course?"

- **Ask ChatGPT for supplementary course materials.** It can be used to create high-quality writing content such as essays, research papers, and blog posts. Educators can enter a topic or keywords and ChatGPT will generate a comprehensive article or blog post, complete with references and supporting evidence.

- **Use ChatGPT to script, edit, and create videos.** It can be used to script and edit videos, such as instructional videos and lectures. Educators can enter a topic or keywords, and ChatGPT will generate a detailed script that will serve as the foundation for the video. It is able to create scripts or content for course videos using screen recording software such as Loom or Screencastify. "Can you make a video script for the second module of my web development course using Loom?" is a prompt example you could use. It can also be used to edit videos, such as by adding captions or subtitles.

- **Have ChatGPT create presentations using Google Slides.** You can request that it create a presentation for your course in Google Slides. "Could you make a presentation for my personal finance course using Google Slides?" is an example of a great prompt to try out. Do note that you will need to integrate ChatGPT with Google Docs. We will see how to do this in Chapter 8.

Marketing Your Course

- **Ask ChatGPT to create landing pages and social media sales copy for your course.** You can request that it create a copy for your course's landing page and social media promotions. "Could you create a landing page and social media copy for my digital marketing course?" is a great prompt to try out.
- **Ask ChatGPT for digital product ideas related to the course.** You can ask it for suggestions on digital products that can be used in conjunction with your course, such as ebooks or workbooks. "Could you recommend some digital products that would complement my mindfulness meditation course?" is an example prompt you could use to get ideas.

Next Steps and Considerations

Increase the Number of Tools in Your Arsenal

While ChatGPT provides numerous content creation options, it is critical to use it in conjunction with other tools and resources. Educators should expand their toolkit to include AI-powered tools such as language translation software and speech recognition software.

Maintain Your Flexibility

Educators must be flexible and adaptable when using ChatGPT and other AI-powered tools. While these tools can be useful, they may not always produce the desired results. It is critical to be willing to make necessary adjustments and changes.

Determine What Artificial Intelligence Is and Is Not Acceptable

Educators should decide which aspects of content creation they want to automate using AI-powered tools and which they want to retain control over. Educators, for example, may prefer to use AI to generate course outlines and quizzes but produce their own instructional videos.

Learn How to Be an Efficient Prompt Engineer

Educators should learn how to prompt and guide the chatbot to generate the desired content. This includes being aware of the technology's limitations and providing clear prompts and parameters.

Use Smart Writing

Educators can use the chatbot's Smart Writing feature to improve their writing skills. Smart Writing provides grammar, syntax, and sentence structure suggestions to help educators create more polished and professional content.

It is truly an exciting and extraordinary piece of AI. It can go beyond just traditional text-related information. We have seen how it can help at different levels of your company or business. Remember that course creation does not only have to be for the educational sector; it can also improve course creation for businesses as well. After all, many companies like to give their employees better opportunities by teaching them new information related to a certain job title and holding workshops that help them improve their knowledge of certain services and job applications.

We have looked at how ChatGPT can help you create content for your courses as well as how to use the software to help come up with an outline for your courses, do video scripting and editing, and come up with the right types of topics and ideas that you could use in order to keep your listeners and readers focused. It can be used for various and enormous workloads, and all of this depends on you and what you need it to do for you.

Now it's time to move on to our next chapter, which speaks about nonfiction and fiction book writing. Try to imagine the all-powerful ChatGPT actually writing a book for you based on what you have already learned about this chatbot. It's already exciting just thinking about it. Well, now that you've created a course, why not get on with making more money by writing a book?

Chapter 7
ChatGPT for Fiction and Nonfiction Writing

The course creator mentioned in an earlier chapter's blog post (Lavern, 2022) used ChatGPT to improve the content of her course by creating titles, descriptions, and outlines. The chatbot, according to the blog post, saved the creator time and energy that would have been spent manually brainstorming ideas and creating outlines. The creator stated that the AI-generated titles and descriptions were so good that they were frequently used as is, with only minor changes.

Furthermore, ChatGPT proved to be a valuable tool for course creators and authors alike. In the case of a course creator, ChatGPT provided fresh and unique ideas that expanded their content creation possibilities. By leveraging ChatGPT's language generation capabilities, the course creator was able to develop more engaging and exciting course materials, leading to increased student engagement and retention rates.

Similarly, ChatGPT can be a game-changer for authors. Once you have created a course, why not venture into writing a book? Whether it's a non-fiction book presenting your ideas or a fictional book inspired by your success story, ChatGPT can assist you in the creative process. It can help generate captivating titles, compelling book descriptions, and detailed outlines, enabling you to craft a book that resonates with readers and showcases your expertise.

With the assistance of ChatGPT, course creators and authors can enhance their content creation endeavors, providing valuable and captivating experiences for their audience. The possibilities are endless, and by embracing ChatGPT's capabilities, you can unlock your creative potential and bring your ideas to life in both educational and literary realms.

Writing Nonfiction Books

When it comes to writing, you can use ChatGPT alongside a writing assistance tool. To do this, you must develop a writing assistant app or a plugin that integrates with word processing software. This includes Microsoft Word or Google Docs. The assistant will then provide suggestions, perform and offer grammar checks, or even help you generate story ideas (Slater, n.d.).

How to Use ChatGPT to Write a Nonfiction Book

There are a few steps you could take to streamline the process and help you write the book you want to write. However, keep in mind that you cannot simply type in the prompt, "Help me write a book on political preferences in the majority today." It will stump the AI because there are too many unknown variables in the prompt, such as your word count and preferred writing style. So, in order to save time and effort, let's go into the steps now (Stark, n.d.).

Steps to Follow

- **Step 1:** Select a topic for your book.
- **Step 2:** Create an outline.
- **Step 3:** Do customer research. You can ask ChatGPT to create a persona for someone interested in reading a book on…
- **Step 4:** Steps 2 and 3 should be repeated until all chapters are finished.
- **Step 5:** Edit and improve the content to fit the structure and style of your book.
- **Step 6:** Before you publish your manuscript, proofread and edit it.

Assume you want to write a nonfiction book about healthy eating habits. It can help you generate ideas for each chapter, such as meal planning, grocery shopping tips, healthy recipes, and the advantages of various food groups. You can then edit and refine the content to fit the structure and style of your book, as well as proofreading the manuscript before publishing.

Creating Nonfiction Book Outlines

There are methods for creating an outline that may or may not correspond to how you write a book. Let's take a look at the steps you could take to get it to create a perfect outline.

Steps to Write a Nonfiction Outline

Step 1: Provide the Niche for Your Book

Personal development, business and entrepreneurship, health and wellness, and history are some niches that exist in the nonfiction book genres. Make sure you know which one your book fits into.

Research and Analyze the Book Market

Before you begin writing your nonfiction book, research the current market to see what similar books are available and identify any gaps or opportunities. It's basic knowledge to do research and find out what's in demand first.

There is one issue that you may face, and this is the fact that ChatGPT may repeat itself or stop writing after some time. For this reason, it is best to do this in small batches. Currently, the AI does not follow word count very well. However, by the time you read this, it may have improved.

Now, you can work with it or create the outline and hire a professional ghostwriter thereafter. If it stops writing midway, always ask it to continue, and not repeat what it has already written.

Consider the following scenario: You want to write a nonfiction book about personal finance. You look around the market and discover that there are many books on budgeting and saving, but few on investing. This assists you in identifying an opportunity to focus your book on investing strategies.

Step 2: Recommend How Many Chapters a New Book Should Have

Based on your research, suggest how many chapters your book should have to provide comprehensive coverage of the topic. For instance, based on your research, you might recommend that a personal finance book contain 10–12 chapters.

Step 3: Set a Word Count

Determine a word count for each chapter based on the overall length of the book and the amount of content required for each chapter. For instance, set a word count of 5,000 words per chapter for a 50,000-word personal finance book with 10 chapters.

Step 4: Create a List of Chapters to the Value Set in Step 2

Create a list of chapter titles and content for each chapter to match the recommended number of chapters. For example, a personal finance book with 10 chapters might include: Introduction to Personal Finance, Setting Financial Goals, Budgeting and Saving, Investing Basics, Retirement Planning, Real Estate Investing, Tax Strategies, Insurance Needs, Estate Planning, and Putting It All Together.

Step 5: Provide a Breakdown of What to Include in Each Chapter, Including a Word Count for Each Section

Make a detailed outline for each chapter, complete with subheadings and word counts for each section. For instance, in the Investing Basics chapter, you could include the following breakdown: Introduction (600 words), Types of Investments (1,500 words), Risks and Returns (500 words), Choosing Investments (1,500 words), and Conclusion (500 words)

Step 6: Provide the Prompts

Prompts for a "personal finance" book can include:

- "What are the benefits of managing personal finances?"
- "How can I grow my finances without the use of a financial advisor?"

Tips for Writing Books

Books are not the same as any other type of material, and this is mainly because of the amount of content in them as well as the market you are writing for. For this reason, before you start writing a book, you should be aware of a few details, some of which include:

- To keep your writing organized and focused, begin with a detailed outline.
- Every day, even if it's only for a few minutes, use ChatGPT to give you points or hints on what you can write about.

- Set goals for yourself, such as a daily word count or a deadline for finishing your manuscript.
- Receiving feedback from others, such as beta readers or an editor, is important.
- Don't be afraid to revise and edit your work several times before publishing it.

Creating Fictional Stories

Now it's time to look at fictional stories and novels (Slater, n.d.).

Steps to Write a Novel Using ChatGPT

Step 1: Instruct the AI

Begin by giving the AI specific instructions about the genre, style, tone, and any other specific elements you want in your novel.

"I want to write a science fiction novel set in the distant future. The tone should be solemn and reflective. You can make plot and character suggestions."

Step 2: Create a World

Create your story's setting by describing the location, time period, and any other relevant details. You can either provide a basic outline or request that the AI generate ideas for you.

"The story takes place in the distant future, after humanity has colonized several planets. The protagonist lives on a space station orbiting a distant planet."

Step 3: Determine a Story Arc

Create a compelling plot with a distinct beginning, middle, and end. You can either provide an outline or ask the AI to generate ideas for you.

"The main character is a scientist who is researching a mysterious alien artifact that has been discovered on the planet's surface," for example. "As the story progresses, they discover secrets about the artifact and the planet's history that endanger the entire human race."

Step 4: List Out the Chapters

Make a list of the chapters you want to include in your novel. This will provide you with a basic framework to work with (Gonsalves, 2023).

Chapter 1: Introduction to the Space Station, Chapter 2: Artifact Discovery, Chapter 3: Research Begins, Chapter 4: Strange Occurrences, Chapter 5: The First Clue, and so on.

Step 5: Create the Characters

Create memorable, one-of-a-kind, and intriguing characters. You can either provide a basic outline or request that the AI generate ideas for you.

For instance, "The main character is Dr. Suarez, a brilliant scientist with a tragic past. She is committed to her work, but she is dealing with the emotional toll of the mission. Other characters that the AI can suggest include her research team, the captain of the space station, and any antagonists that may arise."

Step 6: Detail the Outline of a Chapter

Choose one of your list's chapters and write a detailed outline of what will happen in that chapter. You can give the AI a general outline or ask it to generate ideas.

"Chapter 1: Introduction to the Space Station—Dr. Suarez arrives on the station and meets her team," for example. "She is given a tour of the station and introduced to the captain. She becomes uneasy about the mission and has a nightmare about her past."

Step 7: Drill Down One Chapter's Outline at a Time

Take each chapter and look into the specifics. You can ask the AI to assist you in filling in the blanks or to suggest new ideas.

"In Chapter 1, the AI can suggest more details about the space station, the other characters, and Dr. Suarez's backstory," as an example of a prompt. It can also "suggest ways to add tension and conflict to the scene, such as a malfunction on the station or a disagreement among team members."

Steps 6 and 7 Must Be Repeated

Continue to make detailed outlines for each chapter, delving into the details with the AI's help.

For example, continue to create detailed outlines for each chapter, drilling down into the details with the AI's assistance, and then in Chapter 2, the AI may suggest that "the team discovers the artifact during a dangerous expedition on the planet's surface. They may come across hostile alien creatures or other challenges that heighten the tension in the scene."

Provide Prompts for Each Step

Throughout the process, you can ask the AI to generate new ideas, add details, or help you solve problems. For instance, if you're stuck on a particular scene or need help with a character's development, you can ask the AI for suggestions. You can collaborate with an AI to write a compelling novel by following these steps and working with it as a creative writing partner.

Chapter 8
Generating New Business Ideas Using ChatGPT

Welcome to Chapter 8 of our guide, where we embark on an exhilarating journey into the world of generating new business ideas using ChatGPT. Throughout this guide, you have discovered how ChatGPT can enhance existing businesses, assist in course creation, and even support book writing. Now, in this chapter, we will push the boundaries further and explore how ChatGPT can serve as your creative partner, propelling you towards entrepreneurial success.

With ChatGPT by your side, the possibilities for new business ideas are limitless. Harness its power to brainstorm, innovate, and implement the strategies you have learned in the previous chapters. By tapping into ChatGPT's advanced AI capabilities, you can unlock fresh avenues to generate revenue and leave a lasting impact on the business landscape.

In this chapter, we will share a few ideas to ignite your entrepreneurial spirit and demonstrate the diverse applications of ChatGPT. These ideas serve as a starting point, sparking your imagination and guiding you towards innovative business opportunities. However, remember that the true magic lies in combining ChatGPT's insights with your unique expertise and passion to create something truly exceptional.

Without further ado, here are a few business ideas to explore with ChatGPT:

- **Content writing services:** You could come up with a type of service—for example, a blog or a platform—where you integrate the response system with ChatGPT so that it is able to provide your users with requested content for their blogs, websites, social media posts, and more.
- **CV or resume builder:** You could start a business writing resumes and CVs for your clients, charging a set fee for your service. You can use the AI to come up with information that is directly related to the job description. You can even use the chatbot to write cover letters that are related to the job your client is applying for.
- **Personal coaching platform:** You can create a platform and integrate it with ChatGPT so that it can give advice to each client about their diet, meditation, fitness, and other health-related topics. It can even help your users with daily life coaching tips, motivation, and more.
- **Online tutoring platform:** You can also come up with another platform that is designed to answer student questions about certain topics or subjects related to their schoolwork. You can even go on to cover not only

the school curriculum but professional courses as well. The service can even go so far as to help students with their homework.

- **Market research service:** You can use the chatbot to offer a research service as you collect information from surveys, or you can even get this information from other companies and businesses as well.

- **Social media management and marketing:** You can use the chatbot to come up with content for the services you offer in social media management. This includes coming up with blog posts and creating engaging posts and replies for social media platforms. You can also use it to come up with content for reviewing and recommending different brands that you are marketing through social media. You can even use the chatbot to come up with content for the blogs you are managing.

- **Language translation and editing services:** You can use the chatbot to assist you with an editing and language translation service, as you charge a set fee for each of these services.

- **Virtual Assistant Services:** Offer virtual assistant services to busy professionals and businesses, leveraging ChatGPT to handle administrative tasks, schedule management, email correspondence, and more.

- **E-commerce Product Description Generation:** Provide e-commerce businesses with product description writing services using ChatGPT's language generation capabilities, enabling them to showcase their products effectively.

- **Content Curation and Aggregation:** Create a platform that utilizes ChatGPT to curate and aggregate content from various sources, delivering personalized and relevant content recommendations to users.
- **Travel Planning and Itinerary Services:** Develop a travel planning service where ChatGPT assists travelers in creating personalized itineraries, suggesting destinations, accommodations, and activities based on their preferences.
- **Personalized Gift Recommendation:** Build an online platform powered by ChatGPT to generate personalized gift recommendations for different occasions, considering factors such as recipient's interests, age, and relationship to the gift giver.
- **Event Planning Assistance:** Offer event planning services with ChatGPT as your virtual assistant, helping clients with tasks like venue selection, vendor coordination, and budget management.
- **Language Learning and Practice Platform:** Develop an interactive language learning platform where ChatGPT engages learners in conversational practice, offers language exercises, and provides real-time feedback to improve language skills.
- **Personalized Fitness and Nutrition Coaching:** Create a fitness and nutrition coaching service that integrates ChatGPT to provide tailored workout routines, meal plans, and guidance, empowering individuals to achieve their health goals.
- **Creative Writing Workshops:** Organize creative writing workshops where ChatGPT collaborates with

participants, offering writing prompts, feedback, and inspiration to enhance their writing skills and nurture their creativity.

- **Data Analysis and Visualization Services:** Utilize ChatGPT's ability to analyze data and generate insights to provide data analysis and visualization services to businesses, helping them make informed decisions based on data-driven insights.

- **An all-business-needs assistant:** You can create a service where you provide help to new and upcoming businesses as well as those that have already been in the market for years. You can create brand names and look at phrases using the chatbot. You could also use it to come up with training materials, such as workshop information and content on how to perform certain tasks. Another service you could offer businesses is a feedback analysis where the chatbot will help summarize feedback received from clients.

As you explore the realm of generating new business ideas with ChatGPT, it is essential to approach each idea with thorough research and validation. Take the time to assess market demand, align the ideas with your skills and resources, and understand the needs of your target audience. By leveraging ChatGPT's creative capabilities, these ideas can be transformed into profitable ventures that cater to the evolving needs of your customers.

Remember, the ideas presented in this chapter are merely the beginning. With ChatGPT as your trusted ally, you can venture into uncharted territories, innovating in ways that resonate with your unique skills, interests, and the ever-changing market landscape.

Embrace the power of ChatGPT, tap into your entrepreneurial spirit, and allow your imagination to soar as you embark on a journey to generate new business ideas that hold the potential to transform industries and create a lasting impact. The future is yours to shape, and with ChatGPT as your creative companion, the possibilities are truly boundless.

While exploring new business ideas, it is crucial to conduct adequate research and ensure that your chosen venture is aligned with market demands. ChatGPT will not be liable for any losses incurred, and it is your responsibility to adhere to AI's rules and regulations.

Now that you have gained a comprehensive understanding of ChatGPT and its capabilities, let's delve into the practical aspects of setting it up to connect with your company's platform and unleash its full potential. The next chapter will guide you through the process, empowering you to leverage ChatGPT effectively in your business endeavors.

Your Voice Matters: Ignite the AI Revolution with Your Amazon Review!

If you've been inspired so far, we invite you to be part of the AI revolution. Help us fuel our mission by leaving an empowering review on Amazon. Your feedback not only guides fellow readers but also unlocks the true potential of ChatGPT. Share your insights, experiences, and the impact it has made on your business ventures. Together, let's inspire others to embark on their own AI journey. Leave your review today and join the movement that is shaping the future of AI!

Scan the QR code below for a quick review!

Chapter 9
Setting Up ChatGPT

In light of ChatGPT's record-breaking success as the fastest-growing consumer application in history, this chapter discusses how to use it for business purposes and how you can set it up. According to a Similarweb report (Reuters, 2023), It had over 100 million monthly active users just 2 months after launch, with approximately 13 million unique visitors using the chatbot daily in January. This outpaces other popular apps, such as TikTok and Instagram, which took months or years to reach 100 million users. Now we will look at how businesses can use its popularity to boost customer engagement and overall operations.

It may sound a bit technical at first, but as long as you follow the steps, you will be using ChatGPT in no time (*How #ChatGPT Can Help Your #B2B #Business Reach Its #Goals and #Grow*, 2023).

Steps to Set Up and Use ChatGPT

Here are the steps to follow (Collins, 2023):

Step 1: Register for an OpenAI API Key

You must first obtain an OpenAI API key by visiting the OpenAI website and completing the registration process. This will grant you access to the OpenAI API, which is the foundation of the chatbot.

Step 2: Integrate ChatGPT With Your Platform

Once you have your OpenAI API key, you can integrate it into your platform. This can be done by writing your own integration using the OpenAI API documentation or by using one of the pre-built integrations available on the OpenAI website.

Step 3: Train ChatGPT to Understand Your Business Needs

After integrating it with your platform, you can train it to understand your business requirements. This includes providing it with the necessary data and examples to help it understand your company and the types of questions your customers may have.

Step 4: Customize ChatGPT to Fit Your Brand

ChatGPT can be customized to match the identity of your company by changing its name, appearance, and voice. This will help make your customers' experience much more seamless. It will also aid in the development of your brand recognition.

Step 5 : Test and Refine ChatGPT

After configuring and customizing it, you should thoroughly test it to ensure that it is working properly and providing accurate responses. You can also help it by regularly providing it with new data and examples.

Some Examples

Assume you run an e-commerce site and want to use ChatGPT to assist customers with their purchasing needs. You could integrate it with your platform, train it to understand your product offerings, customize it to fit your brand, and test and refine it to ensure that it is providing accurate responses by following the steps outlined above.

Another scenario is if you run a customer service department and want to use it to handle customer inquiries. You would register for an OpenAI API key, integrate it with your customer service platform, train it to understand common customer inquiries, customize it to fit your brand, and test and refine it to ensure it is providing accurate responses.

ChatGPT for WordPress

You will need the following items to create a ChatGPT chatbot for your WordPress-powered website:

- **A WordPress-based website.** You will need a WordPress-based website to integrate the ChatGPT chatbot. If you don't already have a website, you can create one with WordPress.com or a self-hosted WordPress.org site.

- **An OpenAI account.** To access the GPT-3 API and build the chatbot, you'll also need an OpenAI account. You can create an account on OpenAI's website.

Steps to Build a Chatbot Powered by ChatGPT for Wordpress

Once you have the requirements, you can build your ChatGPT chatbot by following the steps below:

Step 1: Create an OpenAI API Key

Go to the OpenAI website and generate an API key. This key will be required to access the GPT-3 API.

Step 2: Install and Activate the WordPress Plugin

Several WordPress plugins, such as "WP OpenAI Chatbot" or "GPT-3 Chatbot," can be used to integrate the ChatGPT chatbot. Install and activate the desired plugin.

Step 3: Connect Your OpenAI Account

To connect your OpenAI account to the chatbot, enter your OpenAI API key in the plugin settings.

Step 4: Make Your Chatbot Unique.

You can personalize your chatbot by configuring the plugin settings to your preferences. You can, for example, alter the chatbot's name, appearance, and default response.

Step 5: Test Your Chatbot.

After you've customized your chatbot, you can put it to the test by asking it questions and evaluating its responses. You can also improve the chatbot's responses by feeding it more data.

To summarize, creating a ChatGPT chatbot for your WordPress-powered website is relatively simple. You will need a WordPress website and an OpenAI account before you can install a plugin and customize your chatbot. With some testing and fine-tuning, your chatbot can become an excellent addition to your website.

ChatGPT as a Plugin

Another great way to use it is to install it as a plugin. Let's look at two ways you could do this (OpenAI API, n.d.).

Building a Simple To-Do List Plugin With No Authentication

The following steps must be taken:

Step 1: Make a Decision on a Programming Language

Choose a programming language that you are familiar with and that is appropriate for building ChatGPT models. Python is a popular programming language for creating ChatGPT models, and it includes many libraries that can be used to create plugins.

Step 2: Install the Necessary Libraries.

To build your ChatGPT plugin, you will need to install the necessary libraries. The OpenAI API library and the Flask web framework are two libraries that you may require.

Step 3: Create a New ChatGPT Instance.

You must create a new ChatGPT instance after installing the required libraries. You can accomplish this by generating a new API key from the OpenAI dashboard and using it to create a new ChatGPT instance in your code.

Step 4: Define the Plugin Functions.

You will be creating a simple to-do list plugin in this case. Define the plugin functions that will be used by users to add, edit, and delete tasks from their to-do list.

Step 5: Implement the ChatGPT Model.

To make the plugin more user-friendly, you can incorporate the ChatGPT model. This enables the plugin to understand natural language input from the user, allowing users to interact with the plugin more easily.

Step 6: Put the Plugin Through Its Paces.

After you've finished building the plugin, make sure it works properly. You can use the Flask web framework to create a web interface for your plugin, allowing users to interact with it.

Step 7: Make a Record of or Document the Code.

Document your code thoroughly so that other developers can understand how it works and modify it as needed. You can explain the purpose of each function and how it is used with comments and docstrings.

Step 8: Activate the Plugin.

Once you're happy with your plugin, you can share it with others by publishing it to a repository like GitHub. You can also submit it to a package manager like PyPI so that other developers can easily install it.

By following these steps, you will be able to create a simple to-do list plugin that can even be used by other developers as well. Now, let's move on to the next plugin.

Building a Simple To-Do List Plugin With Service Level Automation

The steps for creating this plugin are nearly identical to those mentioned previously (OpenAI API, n.d.). There is simply one more step at the end. After you have chosen a programming language, installed the required libraries, created a new ChatGPT instance, and defined the plugin functions, you can integrate service-level automation to improve the plugin's efficiency. This enables the plugin to automatically add tasks to the user's to-do list in response to certain events, such as the completion of another task or the receipt of an email.

How to Use ChatGPT Integration With Google Docs

- **Step 1:** Go to the add-on option on Google Docs and click on ChatGPT.
- **Step 2:** Once you select ChatGPT, a sidebar will come up, and there you need to put your query.
- **Step 3:** Put up your query on the sidebar and click on the "ask" button.
- **Step 4:** Just copy and paste the output into the Google Doc.

This is how you can integrate ChatGPT to Google Docs.

Now that we've had a look at examples for how to install plugins and integrate the chatbot into your platform, let's move on to the next part of our chapter, which speaks about ChatGPT as a mobile application. Most websites as well as systems and software have been focusing on coming up with mobile apps because the majority of the population prefer to link their devices so that they are able to work from not just their PC, but from their mobile devices as well. The main reason why this is preferred is because we always have our cell phone devices on hand. Should there be any need, we can always open an email, check on sales and revenue, do banking, and so much more from our mobile apps.

ChatGPT as a Mobile Application

As we have seen already, the chatbot is a powerful language model created by OpenAI that can be used for a variety of tasks such as text generation, question answering, and more. It is currently accessible through desktop and mobile browsers, but for the reasons mentioned before about the advantages of using a smartphone, some users may prefer to download and install the app on their local device for a more streamlined experience.

Do note that apps are also able to be downloaded on your local PC as well. This is the main way in which people are able to link their devices and work from anywhere. For example, having your Slack account on your mobile and PC makes it easier to always keep track of what's going on.

How to Install the App

You can visit the link https://www.minitool.com/news/down load-chatgpt.html for detailed instructions for Windows, Mac, and Linux users to download and install the ChatGPT desktop application.

Windows users can simply download the installer file from the website's link, run it, and follow the prompts to complete the installation process.

The installation process is similar for Mac users, but they must download the .dmg file instead. Linux users have a few different options depending on their distribution, but they can generally follow the instructions on the web page to download and install the app. Downloading it from github.com is generally considered safer because the installer is simply a wrapper for the OpenAI ChatGPT website. There is no other data transfer, and users can confirm this by inspecting the source code. However, it is always advisable to proceed with caution and only download software from reputable sources.

It is worth noting that OpenAI has not yet officially released it as a browser extension or mobile app. Third-party apps, such as the ChatGPT Chrome extension, are available and can be downloaded and installed by following the instructions on their website (OpenAI API, n.d.).

Looking at how you can implement it to help with your business or your brand is easier than expected. After all, you can always use the app or a plugin to integrate with your website or blog. This makes it easier for the chatbot to interact with your customers, help you with content creation, and automate certain tasks.

Not an App Person?

If you did not want to integrate the chatbot with your website or blog and were also uninterested in using any of its available apps, then you could always just use the chatbot's website for any information or content creation that you needed. It is easy to use and saves you a lot of time and hassle. But if you want a more personalized experience and a personalized chatbot, then you must integrate it with your company's technology.

If you aren't that great with software or coding, you can always get help from a professional. Or you could always check out the OpenAI website for more information and help on any topic you may be having difficulty with.

An important note for using this chatbot with your business or company is to remember that you must always feed it new information, data, or examples regularly so that it is able to learn and adapt to the movement of your rent or business. Remember that this chatbot will grow as you give it more information, so do this regularly in order for it to keep up with your progress as well as provide your customers with the correct information and help that they will expect.

Now that you understand all of the available methods that you could use to incorporate or integrate it with your business, it's time to move on to our next topic, which revolves around the limitations as well as the ethical considerations that exist for this chatbot. And it may sound a little low after the highs that we have been going through, but with everything out there, there's always a negative aspect. This does not mean that you cannot use the chatbot, but it is information that is necessary to help you understand more about what it cannot do and what you must consider before using this chatbot.

This book was written with the intent of having chatbots assist you with your company, brand, or business, but there are other ways this chatbot has been used inappropriately, and for this reason, certain regulations must be set up. Let's have a look at all of this in more detail in the next chapter.

Chapter 10
Limitations and Ethical Considerations

AI is an incredible type of technology that continues to astound and perplex us with its numerous benefits and applications. The benefits are incredible, and they are all worthwhile. It is important to note that you should give AI a chance. Regardless, it is critical that you understand the limitations and ethical considerations of ChatGPT and other AI. You will be able to use it to the best of your ability if you understand what it can and cannot do.

The Orissa Post (Network, 2023) article highlights how cybercriminals are quick to adopt new technologies, such as ChatGPT, for their malicious activities. The article provides one example of how cybercriminals use it to conduct phishing attacks.

Phishing is a type of social engineering attack in which cybercriminals use deception to trick users into disclosing sensitive information such as usernames, passwords, or credit card information. It can be used by cybercriminals to build convincing chatbots that impersonate legitimate organizations or individuals, such as banks or government agencies, in order to trick users into disclosing personal information. It may sound scary but it is true. There has also been a lot of information about scams that have been going around. Most of them are considered a type of phishing, and if scammers use ChatGPT to operate, this will put a lot of people at risk.

A cybercriminal, for example, could use it to create a chatbot that mimics a bank's customer service representative. When a user contacts the chatbot with a request, the chatbot may respond with a prompt requesting sensitive information such as the user's account number and password. The chatbot could use pre-programmed responses to make the conversation appear more convincing and natural, making the user less likely to notice the scam.

The use of the chatbot for phishing attacks emphasizes the importance of businesses being aware of potential risks and taking appropriate measures to protect their customers. This includes educating users about the dangers of phishing and implementing strong security measures to protect sensitive information, such as multi-factor authentication and encryption.

It is critical to understand that as AI technology such as ChatGPT advances, so will the risks and threats associated with it. As a result, it is critical to be proactive in ensuring that AI is developed and used in an ethical and responsible manner, with appropriate safeguards in place to protect users from potential harm.

Limitations of ChatGPT

Let's look at some of the limitations you could experience when using the chatbot. Remember that this is a learning AI, and in the near future, most of its limitations will be overcome. The chatbot will eventually learn to overcome these limitations (Vasylkiv, 2023).

- **Limited understanding of context and background information.** Assume a user inquires about a specific restaurant through the chatbot. ChatGPT may provide information about the location, menu, and reviews of the restaurant. Despite this, it may be unable to comprehend the user's context or preferences, such as whether the user is looking for a family-friendly restaurant or a romantic dinner destination.
- **Lack of common sense and general knowledge.** Its responses are generated based on the patterns it has discovered while training on massive amounts of text. As a result, it may lack the common sense and general knowledge that humans possess. For instance, a user might ask, "Can I put my laptop in the oven?" It may fail to recognize that this is an absurd question and respond with a factual response, potentially causing the user to damage their laptop.
- **Limited ability to understand and respond to complex questions.** The complexity of the question posed limits its responses. If a user asks a complex question that requires a deep understanding of a specific domain or specialized knowledge, it may be

unable to provide an accurate or useful answer. For example, if a user requests that it explain the complexities of quantum mechanics, it may be unable to provide a comprehensive or accurate explanation.

- **Unnatural due to lack of divergent thinking.** The responses of the chatbot are generated by a machine learning algorithm that mimics human language patterns, but they are still unnatural and lack the divergent thinking and creativity that humans have. It, for example, may be unable to respond to a user's comment or question in a witty or humorous manner.

- **Detectable as non-human.** Although its responses are sophisticated, they are still generated by a machine and can be identified as non-human by careful observation or scrutiny. For example, if a user asks it to identify the emotions conveyed by a piece of music, it may be unable to provide a response that reflects human emotions and understanding.

- **Difficulty in understanding sarcasm and irony.** It may have difficulty understanding sarcasm and irony in a user's comments or questions, resulting in inaccurate or inappropriate responses. For example, if a user asks sarcastically if the AI can predict the winning lottery numbers, it may respond factually without detecting the sarcasm.

- **Too detailed and comprehensive.** its responses may be overly detailed and comprehensive, which can be overwhelming or unhelpful to users. For example, if a user asks for a simple pancake recipe, it may respond with a detailed recipe that includes many unnecessary steps and ingredients.

- **Biased to be formal.** Its responses are intended to be neutral and formal, which may not always be appropriate or desirable in a conversational context. If a user asks it for ideas on a fun activity to do with friends, it may respond in a formal and generic manner, such as suggesting going to the movies or a restaurant.

Overall, while it can be a useful tool in many situations, it is critical to be aware of its limitations and use it appropriately.

Ethical Considerations

There are also ethical considerations associated with the use of ChatGPT (Pereira, 2023):

- **Bias in training data.** One of the primary concerns with it is the possibility of bias in the training data used to train the model. If the training data is biased towards or against a particular group or perspective, the resulting chatbot's responses may be biased as well. For example, if a chatbot is trained using data that only reflects the experiences of a specific demographic group, it may be unable to provide helpful responses to people from other backgrounds.
- **Misuse and abuse of the technology.** Another ethical consideration is the possibility of technology misuse and abuse. Chatbots, for example, could be used to manipulate or deceive people, or they could be used to

spread misinformation. A malicious actor, for example, could use a chatbot to impersonate someone else and carry out fraudulent activities.

- **Impact on job displacement and loss of human interaction.** The widespread use of chatbots powered by GPT technology may result in the displacement of human workers in certain industries. Chatbots, for example, could replace customer service representatives, resulting in job losses for those employees. Furthermore, the use of chatbots may result in a loss of human interaction and connection, as people may choose to interact with chatbots rather than real people.

- **Privacy and security concerns.** ChatGPT technology could also raise concerns about privacy and security. Chatbots, for example, may collect personal information about users that can be used for targeted advertising or other purposes. Furthermore, if a chatbot is compromised, sensitive information about users may be exposed.

- **Responsibility of developers, users, and society.** Finally, the responsibility for ensuring that ChatGPT technology is used ethically falls on multiple parties, including developers, users, and society as a whole. Developers are responsible for ensuring that their chatbots are designed and trained in an ethical manner, while users are responsible for using chatbots in an appropriate and ethical manner. The impact of chatbots on employment, privacy, and other important issues must be considered by society as a whole, and steps must be taken to mitigate any negative effects.

Limitations for Marketers

ChatGPT, as a language model, has some limitations when it comes to business and marketing applications. This is the main reason why there is always a need for someone to oversee the chatbot and ensure that everything is accurate and in order. Let's look at what the chatbot is unable to do for marketers now (Staff, 2023).

- **It cannot perform physical tasks.** It is a digital tool that can only interact with users via text or voice conversations. It is unable to carry out physical tasks such as packaging, shipping, or delivering goods. For example, if a customer orders a product and requests that it be shipped to their location, it can assist with the ordering process but cannot physically pack and deliver the product.
- **It is not 100% accurate.** Although it is a highly advanced language model, it is not completely accurate. It may not understand certain contexts or provide incorrect information based on the data on which it was trained. As a result, marketers cannot rely on it alone to provide accurate information or insights. Because of a lack of context or incomplete data, it, for example, may provide incorrect pricing information for a product.

- **It is not a substitute for human decision-making.** While it can provide data-driven insights and recommendations, it cannot replace human decision-making. When making business decisions, marketers must take into account a variety of factors such as brand values, customer preferences, and industry trends. ChatGPT may be unable to account for all of these variables while providing insights. It, for example, may suggest a marketing campaign that contradicts a brand's values or does not resonate with the target audience.

To summarize, it has limitations in terms of performing physical tasks, accuracy, and human decision-making. Marketers must be aware of all of these limitations so that they can use ChatGPT as a tool to assist their decision-making rather than relying on it entirely.

A Call for Responsible Use of AI

AI technology has enormous potential to transform industries and improve people's lives. However, it also presents significant challenges. These may sound a bit daunting, but remember that the AI is continually learning and evolving. It will eventually be able to overcome its limitations. Let's look at some of these regulations now (Lekhraj, 2023).

- **Plagiarism.** AI can be used to create fake content that is difficult to distinguish from real content, such as essays, articles, and even videos. This could result in plagiarism and intellectual property infringement. It is something that most people have an issue with today, but it does always tell its users to make sure that they aren't plagiarizing any content and to always do research before publishing anything first.

- **Misrepresentation.** AI can be used to generate false profiles or misleading information, resulting in reputational damage and harm to individuals and organizations.
- **Privacy violations.** AI has the potential to collect and process massive amounts of personal data, raising concerns about privacy and data protection.
- **Undetermined accountability.** AI can make significant decisions, but it can be difficult to determine who is responsible for those decisions.
- **Bias and discrimination.** Artificial intelligence algorithms have the potential to be biased or discriminatory, perpetuating existing social and economic inequalities.
- **Massive capability overhang.** AI's capabilities are rapidly advancing, and it may soon outperform human intelligence in many areas, raising concerns about its potential impact on society and the economy.
- **Limited governance.** AI governance and regulation are currently lacking, which could lead to unintended consequences and negative outcomes.
- **Unclear copyright and other legal liabilities.** The use of AI-generated content raises concerns about intellectual property and other legal liabilities.

- **Erosion of customer trust.** If AI is misused or produces incorrect results, it can erode customer trust and harm a company's reputation.
- **Environmental impact.** The energy consumption of AI systems, as well as the materials used to build them, may have a significant environmental impact.
- **Centralizing power at the top.** It has the potential to concentrate power and wealth in the hands of a few large corporations and individuals, resulting in new forms of inequality and monopoly.

Potential Regulations for AI

To address these issues, there is an increasing call for AI regulation. Let's have a look at some of the potential regulations (Simons, 2023).

Developer Regulation

AI developers should be "ethical by design," which means that ethical considerations should be integrated into AI system development from the start. This could include developing ethical guidelines for AI developers and mandating transparency in AI decision-making processes.

Privacy and GDPR

Data protection laws, such as the EU's General Data Protection Regulation (GDPR), should be required of AI developers. This could include ensuring that AI systems are built to protect personal data and that individuals have the ability to access, correct, or delete their data.

A Debate Is on the Horizon

The question of how artificial intelligence should be regulated is still being debated. Some argue that AI should be regulated in the same way that pharmaceuticals and financial services are. Others argue that artificial intelligence is still in its early stages and that regulation could stifle innovation and growth. Finally, as technology advances and its impact on society becomes clearer, the debate over AI regulation will almost certainly continue.

After taking into account all of the limitations and ethical concerns surrounding it, it is critical that we, as users, understand why the chatbot was created and what it can and cannot do. Every tool, like any other in the world, has benefits and drawbacks. As a result, as humans with intelligence and understanding of how the world works, as well as moralistic values, we must ensure that we use all technology to benefit everyone, including ourselves, but without malicious intent. We should never use technology to defame others or to engage in unjust or illegal behavior.

Another critical point is to acknowledge its limitations. We must accept that while AI is a fantastic tool, there are some things it cannot do. Although it is referred to as "artificial intelligence," it is not the same as human intelligence. It will never truly comprehend emotions, at least not yet. As a result, AI and the ChatGPT chatbot will be biased at times. It will never get your sarcasm or clever jokes. It will be a logical and straightforward machine that will be unable to share any humor with you until it learns how. And this may take longer than some would like.

All of this demonstrates the distinction between AI and human beings. This is the primary reason why AI will never truly be able to replace humans. Although AI can perform tasks more accurately and efficiently, it lacks the human and emotional elements that come from humans. However, we should never assume that AI will always be 100% accurate. It, too, is in the learning stages, and some of the information it will provide on certain topics may be inaccurate. If you visit the ChatGPT website, you will also be notified of anything that it may not be aware of or have all of the information on. Remember that it is a language model that was designed to also learn from you, the user.

Now that you are aware of all of the limitations of the chatbot, it is time to move on to the next topic, which discusses the future of this amazing technology... Let's take a look at what's next in the world of AI.

Chapter 11
A Brighter Future Ahead

ChatGPT and other AI technologies, particularly in the context of business, have the potential to provide convenience and improve our lives. While there are issues with AI, such as privacy violations and bias, there is also an increasing call for responsible AI use and regulation. Ultimately, the goal of AI is not to replace humans, but to assist us in creating a more livable society and a higher quality of life.

BuiltIn's article *The Artificial Intelligence Future: How Will AI Impact Our Lives?* provides a comprehensive overview of the potential applications of AI in various industries as well as the ethical considerations associated with its development and use (BuiltIn, 2021).

The Future of ChatGPT and AI Development

ChatGPT's future will be a significant advancement over the GPT-3 language model. We've seen how far it's already come, and we've briefly mentioned the newer model, but GPT-4 is up next in our AI superhero league. This model is superior in that it can process both visual and textual information and respond with support and content (Wong, 2022).

Why ChatGPT Is Opening up the Paths for More Development in AI

- **ChatGPT has brought us one step closer to true artificial intelligence.** It represents a significant advancement in the development of natural language processing technology, which is a key component of artificial intelligence. It moves us closer to the goal of creating intelligent machines that can communicate with humans on a human-like level by allowing users to interact with a machine in a more natural way.
- **GPT-3 gives AI innovators a great platform to work with.** GPT-3 is one of the most advanced NLP models currently available, and it provides developers and researchers with a powerful tool for exploring the potential of AI. GPT-3's ability to generate highly realistic and coherent language opens up new possibilities in areas such as chatbots, virtual assistants, and language translation.
- **ChatGPT is driving a healthy debate on the AI we want to create.** The advancement of artificial intelligence is not without its challenges and controversies, and it is contributing to a healthy debate about the ethical and social implications of this technology. As AI advances and becomes more

integrated into our lives, it is critical to consider questions such as: What kind of AI do we want to create? How can we ensure that artificial intelligence benefits society as a whole? GPT-3 and its successors are assisting in the advancement of these discussions.

- **ChatGPT and its successors are a cause for optimism.** While there are risks associated with AI development, there are also numerous reasons to be optimistic about its potential to improve our lives. It is just one example of the kinds of breakthroughs that are possible, and it's exciting to imagine what might be possible in the coming years and decades.

What ChatGPT Means for the Future of Business

- **The democratization of AI in the near future.** ChatGPT and similar NLP models have the potential to democratize access to AI technology, allowing businesses of all sizes to benefit from this powerful tool. A small startup, for example, may be able to use it to create a chatbot that can answer customer inquiries without requiring a large team of developers or a large budget. This can help to level the playing field and create more opportunities for innovation.
- **A natural language interface.** As it and other NLP models advance, they are increasingly being used to provide natural language interfaces for a wide range of applications. For example, a virtual assistant powered by ChatGPT could assist employees in navigating

complex software systems, reducing the need for extensive training and increasing productivity.

- **The lowering of entry barriers.** Previously, developing AI applications necessitated specialized knowledge and substantial resources. ChatGPT and other advanced NLP models, on the other hand, are making it easier for businesses to develop AI-powered applications without having to understand the underlying technology in-depth. This can help to open up new avenues for innovation in areas such as customer service, marketing, and product development.
- **Driving innovation in the medium term.** ChatGPT and other AI technologies are likely to drive innovation across a wide range of industries. For example, new types of virtual assistants that are more human-like and capable of handling complex tasks may emerge. Alternatively, we may see the emergence of new applications in fields such as healthcare, where AI has the potential to revolutionize diagnosis and treatment.

The possibilities are limitless, and it is only the start of what promises to be an exciting journey.

GPT-4

OpenAI's GPT-4 language model is the next generation of language models. It is referred to as a "monster" due to its anticipated size and capabilities (Bastian, 2022). Here are some details about GPT-4:

What is GPT-4 and How Will It Boost Business Growth?

GPT-4 is a language model that processes and generates human-like language using deep learning algorithms. It is capable of tasks such as language translation, text summarization, and conversation generation.

GPT-4 is expected to have a significant impact on the market for AI-based language technologies. GPT-4 is expected to help businesses grow by enabling more advanced language-based AI applications like chatbots, virtual assistants, and automated customer service systems. A company, for example, can use GPT-4 to build a chatbot capable of handling complex customer inquiries and providing personalized recommendations. GPT-4 could have new use cases in industries like healthcare and finance, where accurate and natural language processing is critical.

What's New in GPT-4?

It is larger and thus will require more computer power than the previous models. It can understand more complex language and perform a much larger range of tasks. You will not need to put in as many prompts, as it is able to better understand you than the other models.

GPT-4 is expected to implement sparsity, which will make it more efficient and faster than all of the previous models. It will also have improved AI alignment, so it is more aligned with human values and goals. It may be able to generate more accurate language translations, while its reduced need for prompting may make it easier to use for chatbot development.

When Will It Be Released?

GPT-4 is operational and currently in use, with this instance being a demonstration of the model. As of now, OpenAI has announced plans to publish a paper on GPT-4 sometime in 2023. This does not imply that GPT-4 is still in its developmental stages: it does exist and it is publicly accessible. However, specific accessibility options, including potential paid subscriptions, are determined by OpenAI and may vary.

To summarize, the possibilities are limitless, and any industry will be able to benefit from the abilities and functions provided by these GPT language models. The sky's the limit as long as you know what you want to do with AI and how it can benefit you, your content, your company, and your employees.

These language models will continue to improve, and their limitations will diminish over time as they adapt to human needs, learning to be less biased and more empathic. Content will be generated more quickly, and there will be no need to be as concise as possible. With GPT-4's success and evolution to process more, we can already see that AI in GPT models is impressively progressing. The future looks promising. Let's look forward to it.

Conclusion

ChatGPT is a marvelous and revolutionary form of technology that is constantly changing the way we, as humans, react to and interact with today's machines. This artificial intelligence language model, which was built on the GPT-3.5 system, was and continues to be trained on massive amounts of data. All of this aids it in understanding and responding to natural language input.

The AI has been used and applied in a variety of industries thus far. It has been demonstrated time and again that ChatGPT is beneficial to businesses looking to save money and time. Reading this book has given you information about the numerous applications that it has for both large and small businesses.

We looked at how artificial intelligence has progressed from its inception as an afterthought to what it is today. From machines that simply followed their programming to language models that can understand prompts and questions and respond with factual and accurate content, we've come a long way.

This AI chatbot is a fantastic piece of technology for any company looking to thrive in today's market. It can automate the majority of a company's routine tasks by using prompt engineering. Its business applications range from research compilation to marketing content creation, brainstorming ideas for your sales and business, and even writing computer code. We also investigated how ChatGPT can provide after-sales support and translate text for your customer service. Using its automation capabilities, the software can streamline and improve all processes.

And, of course, it can make money for your company. Remember that you can use specific prompts to assist your business with lead generation as well as idea generation. ChatGPT can boost sales by providing personalized recommendations to your customers. It is useful for marketing and analyzing data such as customer behavior, what drives sales, and what you can do to improve your product's image—or your company and brand image—resulting in increased profits.

These use cases show how much the AI can benefit your business or company. To summarize, ChatGPT is a powerful piece of technology with the potential to transform businesses and industries in almost every way. It is wise and profitable to use artificial intelligence to automate tasks and improve customer service. Reducing the need for human intervention can save you a significant amount of time and money.

This does not imply that the human workforce will be phased out. When AI was first considered, the researchers who came up with the idea wanted to create something that would help the human workforce with as much of the workload as possible so that they could focus on more complex systems and devices. As a result, it has demonstrated today that it is available to improve services, provide us with content quickly and efficiently, and carry out responsibilities that would have taken the human workforce a long time to complete. It's not because it gets rid of them, but because it allows them to concentrate on more complex tasks instead.

The future of this AI is exciting. It is only natural for all businesses and industries to eventually incorporate an AI as powerful as ChatGPT into their systems. When it comes to AI, there will always be growth and innovation, and ChatGPT shows us that this is only the beginning. When it comes to what this AI can do, there is so much to discover.

So, step boldly into this captivating realm, where human ingenuity merges with artificial intelligence to redefine the very fabric of business. The future awaits, and ChatGPT will be there, guiding you every step of the way. The future is now, and it's time to embark on an extraordinary adventure where dreams become reality.

Bonus

Unleashing the Power of AI - 200 Prompts for Business Owners & Entrepreneurs with ChatGPT

Navigate the business landscape with the help of AI - this bonus provides a comprehensive list of prompts to spark dynamic and insightful conversations with ChatGPT, your digital business advisor. Be prepared to transform your entrepreneurial journey with this powerful tool!

Thank You for Being a Part of the AI Revolution!

Leave Your Review on Amazon Today!

As you reach the end of "Unleashing the Millionaire Power of ChatGPT," we want to express our sincere gratitude for joining us on this transformative AI journey. We hope that the insights, strategies, and possibilities shared in this book have empowered you to harness the true potential of ChatGPT in your business and creative endeavors.

Your feedback is invaluable to us. By leaving a review on Amazon, you play a pivotal role in shaping the future of AI and guiding others in their exploration of ChatGPT. Share your thoughts, experiences, and the impact this book has had on your understanding of artificial intelligence. Your review will inspire fellow readers and contribute to the vibrant community of AI enthusiasts and entrepreneurs.

We appreciate the time and commitment you have invested in reading "Unleashing the Millionaire Power of ChatGPT." Now, let your voice be heard and leave your review on Amazon. Together, let's propel the AI revolution forward and unlock new horizons of success and innovation. Thank you for being a part of this extraordinary journey!

Scan the QR code below for a quick review!

References

Ahmed, Z. (2023, February 22). *We asked ChatGPT if it will replace content creators and programmers: This is what the chatbot said.* The Indian Express. https://indianexpress.com/article/technology/tech-news-technology/asking-chatgpt-if-it-will-replace-content-creators-programmers-8461241/

Application of AI. (n.d.). Www.javatpoint.com. https://www.javatpoint.com/application-of-ai

Bastian, M. (2022, December 26). *ChatGPT is just a taste of a "monster" GPT-4 says Gary Marcus.* THE DECODER. https://the-decoder.com/gpt-4-will-be-a-monster-and-chatgpt-just-the-foretaste

Bednarski, D. (2023, January 24). *What is OpenAI? - Its History and How It Is Changing the World.* Taskade Blog. https://www.taskade.com/blog/openai-chatgpt-history/

Built In. (2021, September 17). *Artificial Intelligence: The Future is Here.* https://builtin.com/artificial-intelligence/artificial-intelligence-future

Butler, S. (2023, March 31). *GPT 3.5 vs. GPT 4: What's the Difference?* How-to Geek. https://www.howtogeek.com/882274/gpt-3-5-vs-gpt-4/

Cerullo, M. (2021, January 14). *How AI-powered chatbots could be job killers.* CBS News. https://www.cbsnews.com/news/chatgpt-chatbot-artificial-intelligence-job-replacement/

Collins, B. (2023, February 18). *How To Build A ChatGPT Chatbot For Your Website In Minutes.* Forbes. https://www.forbes.com/sites/barrycollins/2023/02/18/how-to-build-a-chatgpt-chatbot-for-your-website-in-minutes/?sh=23bd762d4db8

Fishbowl Insights. (2022, March 7). *ChatGPT Sees Strong Early Adoption in the Workplace.* https://www.fishbowlapp.com/insights/chatgpt-sees-strong-early-adoption-in-the-workplace

Gilmore, D., Nottingham, A., & Zerwes, M. (2023, February 10). *ChatGPT and learning design: what online content creation opportunities does it offer?* THE Campus Learn, Share, Connect. https://www.timeshighereducation.com/campus/chatgpt-and-learning-design-what-online-content-creation-opportunities-does-it-offer

Gonsalves, R. A. (2023, February 4). *Using ChatGPT as a Creative Writing Partner — Part 1: Prose.* Medium. https://towardsdatascience.com/using-chatgpt-as-a-creative-writing-partner-part-1-prose-dc9a9994d41f

Gungor, A. (2023, March 22). *ChatGPT: What Are Hallucinations And Why Are They A Problem For AI Systems.* Bernard Marr. https://bernardmarr.com/chatgpt-what-are-hallucinations-and-why-are-they-a-problem-for-ai-systems/

How #ChatGPT Can Help Your #B2B #Business Reach Its #Goals And #Grow. (2023, February 9). Www.linkedin.com. https://www.linkedin.com/pulse/how-chatgpt-can-help-your-b2b-business-reach-its-goals-grow-lakeb2b

How Does Chat GPT Work? (2023, Jan 5). ATRIA Innovation. www.atriainnovation.com/en/how-does-chat-gpt-work/

Hu, K. (2023, February 1). *ChatGPT sets record for fastest-growing user base: analyst note.* Reuters. https://www.reuters.com/technology/chatgpt-sets-record-fastest-growing-user-base-analyst-note-2023-02-01/

Hunt, S. (2021, September 27). *Trends in Artificial Intelligence (AI) in Cybersecurity.* Datamation. https://www.datamation.com/security/artificial-intelligence-ai-in-cybersecurity-trends/

IndustryTrends. (2023, February 7). *ChatGPT For Lead Generation - A Complete Guide.* Analytics Insight. https://www.analyticsinsight.net/chatgpt-for-lead-generation-a-complete-guide/

Kleinman, Z. (2023, February 6). *"Google killer" ChatGPT sparks AI chatbot race.* BBC News. https://www.bbc.com/news/technology-64538604

Lavern, R. (2022, January 31). *How ChatGPT Helped a Course Creator Thrive.* Rachel Lavern. https://rachellavern.com/blog/how-chatgpt-helped-a-course-creator-thrive/

Lee, A. (2023, January 26). *What Are Large Language Models Used For and Why Are They Important?* NVIDIA Blog. https://blogs.nvidia.com/blog/2023/01/26/what-are-large-language-models-used-for/

Lekhraj, T. (2023, January 19). *What ChatGPT Reveals About the Urgent Need for Responsible AI.* BCG Henderson Institute. https://bcghendersoninstitute.com/what-chatgpt-reveals-about-the-urgent-need-for-responsible-ai/

Martindale, J. (2023, May 11). *What is Google Bard? Here's everything you need to know.* ZDNET. https://www.zdnet.com/article/what-is-google-bard-heres-everything-you-need-to-know/

McDonald, A. (2022, December 18). ChatGPT: *Building an Online Course Using AI. Geek Culture.* https://medium.com/geekculture/chatgpt-building-an-online-course-using-ai-31020827d76f

Mehdi, Y. (2023, February 7). *Reinventing search with a new AI-powered Microsoft Bing and Edge, your copilot for the web.* The Official Microsoft Blog. https://blogs.microsoft.com/blog/2023/02/07/reinventing-search-with-a-new-ai-powered-microsoft-bing-and-edge-your-copilot-for-the-web/

Mohmad, P. (2023, January 31). *Top 10 Productive Use Cases of ChatGPT for the Year 2023.* Analytics Insight. https://www.analyticsinsight.net/top-10-productive-use-cases-of-chatgpt-for-the-year-2023/

Network, P. N. (2023, February 19). *From social media to ChatGPT, cyber criminals quick to adopt new tech.* Odisha News, OrissaPOST. https://www.orissapost.com/from-social-media-to-chatgpt-cyber-

Nosewiczj. (2023, February 1). *Using ChatGPT in Market Research.* Clear Seas Research. https://clearseasresearch.com/blog/artificial-intelligence/using-chatgpt-in-market-research/

Objartel, M. (2023, March 20). *ChatGPT for Customer Service: Limitations, Capabilities, and Prompts.* Klaus. https://www.klausapp.com/blog/chatgpt-for-customer-service/

OpenAI API. (n.d.). Platform.openai.com. https://platform.openai.com/docs/plugins/examples

Ortiz, J. (2023, March 2). *Maximize Your Content Creation Strategy With ChatGPT.* Beehiiv Blog. https://blog.beehiiv.com/p/maximize-your-content-creation-strategy-with-chatgpt

Pereira, B. P. (2023, February 5). *ChatGPT: Ethical Concerns of Generative AI Models Persist.* CIO.inc. https://www.cio.inc/chatgpt-ethical-concerns-generative-ai-models-persist-a-21116

Sanchez, S. (2022, December 21). *Maximizing Productivity with ChatGPT and Automation.* DeepIdea Lab. https://www.deepidealab.com/maximizing-productivity-with-chatgpt-and-automation/

Schmid, S. (2022, December 8). *Write the perfect ChatGPT prompts in 5 easy steps!* Neuroflash. https://neuroflash.com/blog/chatgpt-how-to-write-the-perfect-prompts/

Schroer, A. (2023, March 3). *What is Artificial Intelligence? How Does AI Work?* Built In. BuiltIn. https://builtin.com/artificial-intelligence

Simons, J. (2023, February 5). *The Creator of ChatGPT Thinks AI Should Be Regulated.* Time. https://time.com/6252404/mira-murati-chatgpt-openai-interview/

Slater, D. (n.d.). *How to Use Chat GPT to Write a Novel.* GripRoom. https://

www.griproom.com/fun/how-to-use-chat-gpt-to-write-a-novel

Staff, Entrepreneur. (2023, February 16). *How Can Marketers Use ChatGPT? Here Are the Top 11 Uses.* Entrepreneur. www.entrepreneur.com/science-technology/how-can-marketers-use-chatgpt-here-are-the-top-11-uses/445015

Stark, A. (n.d.). *How to Use ChatGPT to Write Non-Fiction Books.* GripRoom. https://www.griproom.com/fun/how-to-use-chatgpt-to-write-non-fiction-books

Tanner, D. (2023, January 19). *ChatGPT: Your New Social Media Marketing Secret Weapon.* Social Media College. https://www.socialmediacollege.com/blog/open-ai-chat-gpt/

UXDA. (2022, January 26). *UX Case Study: Applying ChatGPT User Experience to Banking.* Www.theuxda.com. https://www.theuxda.com/blog/ux-case-study-applying-chatgpt-user-experience-banking

Vasylkiv, B. (2023, January 25). *Limitations and Ethical Considerations of Using ChatGPT.* Incora - European Software Development Company. https://incora.software/insights/chatgpt-limitations

Wafeq. (2023). *The 11 Best Ways of Using ChatGPT for Business.* https://www.wafeq.com/en/business-hub/for-business/the-11-best-ways-of-using-chatgpt-for-business

Wong, J. (2022, December 15). *Three reasons why ChatGPT makes GPT-4 really exciting.* LinkedIn. https://www.linkedin.com/pulse/three-reasons-why-chatgpt-makes-gpt-4-really-exciting-jeff-wong

Yalalov, D. (2022, December 11). *100 Best ChatGPT Prompts to Unleash AI's Potential.* Metaverse Post. https://mpost.io/100-best-chatgpt-prompts-to-unleash-ais-potential/